Picture Book Story Hours

Picture Book Story Hours

From Birthdays to Bears

Paula Gaj Sitarz

Libraries Unlimited, Inc.
Littleton, Colorado
1987

LIBRARIES UNLIMITED, INC.
P.O. Box 6633
Englewood, CO 80155-6633

Library of Congress Cataloging-in-Publication Data

Sitarz, Paula Gaj, 1955-
   Picture book story hours.

   Bibliography: p. 185
   Includes index.
   1. Story-telling. 2. Picture-books for children.
I. Title.
LB1140.35.S76S57 1986   372.6'4   86-21439
ISBN 0-87287-556-3

To Michael, Andrew, Mom, and Jane

Contents

THE PROGRAM PLANS

Acknowledgments

I am grateful to the children's staffs of the Thomas Crane Public Library, Quincy, Massachusetts, the Southworth Library, South Dartmouth, Massachusetts, and the New Bedford Free Public Library, New Bedford, Massachusetts, for their assistance.

Introduction

"This is my first year doing story hour. What works?"

"I don't have much time to plan story hour. What should I do?"

"Do preschoolers enjoy a story hour on giants?"

"I'm bored with this program outline. There must be another way to do a story hour on bears."

"Sure, I'll do story hour while you're on vacation. Just leave a program plan."

Sound familiar?

If you're doing story hours for the first time . . .

If you have little time to prepare programs . . .

If you're afraid to try an untested program plan . . .

If you'd like to present a program subject in a new way . . .

If you're asked to do a story hour for someone . . .

The story hour program plans in this book will help.

For six years I've done story hours with four- and five-year-old youngsters at the Thomas Crane Public Library in Quincy, Massachusetts. I've worked with many groups of preschoolers: those who attend the picture book story hour which runs from October to May; those who attend summer programs;

and those who visit from nursery and preschools. Successful stories and activities have remained in my repertoire. Less successful stories and activities have been dropped.

I've tried various formats, explored many story hour subjects, and consulted other experienced children's librarians. I've spent hours searching shelves, consulting professional resources, thumbing through card catalogs, and hunting down books in other libraries. I've agonized over whether the children would enjoy a certain story or activity and if the order in which I presented the material would work.

The result of these efforts is the twenty-two tested story hour program plans you find in this book. They are easy to do and in most cases involve no cost. As for running time: everyone reads at a different pace, of course, and audience participation definitely impacts time, but in general the programs outlined here take between thirty and forty-five minutes each.

The first chapter, "Putting It Together," is a guide to selecting, organizing, preparing, executing, and evaluating material for story hours. You'll also find information about location and space requirements, registration, publicity, and programs for parents.

Each program plan is preceded by publicity ideas. If you're doing a series of programs, you won't need to publicize each one, but if you use any of these programs during the summer or during a vacation week, then you might want to publicize it individually.

Within each program plan, you'll find ways to introduce your read alouds and other material, actual book talks that vary in length, and suggestions on how to use other material in the program. Fingerplays and action rhymes are reprinted in the program plans. The plans are followed by "Try This!" a selective list of other books to read aloud and other material options: book talks, other story forms, poetry, participation books, fingerplays and action rhymes, songs, filmstrips, films, and activities. Full bibliographic information is given for each item, and I've indicated if a title is wordless or nonfiction or if it works well as a felt board story.

The final chapter, "Resources and Aids," is an annotated list of books that will also help you plan and execute your programs.

Out-of-print books, as well as books in print, are included in the text because most library collections have a good selection of both. Books also go out of print at a moment's notice, and they can just as quickly be reissued or reprinted. If a title is not readily available, request it from another library.

Use the program plans as is, or use them as a starting point, a springboard to adapt to your particular needs. Modify the plans using your own ideas or using some of the other materials suggested for each topic. Delete, alter, lengthen, shorten, or rearrange as needed. If you have three year olds in your story hour, substitute some of the shorter book titles listed in "Try This!"

Whether the topic is magic, music, or mice, you're sure to find a subject in the pages that follow to please those eager preschoolers!

Putting
It Together

SELECTING MATERIAL

Do you remember when your English teacher gave you an assignment to write a report? If the teacher didn't suggest a topic, you agonized over what you should write. The same is true when planning story hours. It's much easier to plan a program if you select a subject and choose material related to it. Don't pick too narrow a topic though. If you do, you might use some titles of inferior quality merely because you need material to fit your subject.

Select topics that interest and are within the understanding of children ages four and five. Ideal subjects include the family, friends, seasons, food, colors, holidays, and animals.

The main goals of the story hour are to bring children's literature of artistic and literary merit to youngsters and to have children view books and reading as pleasurable experiences. Thus, reading aloud is the focus of the picture book story hour.

The only way to find appropriate books to read aloud is to read widely, from several library collections. Use published book lists, retrospective and current, to point you toward good titles. Review sources keep you abreast of what's being published and help you eliminate titles not worth considering. The primary journals are *School Library Journal*, *The Horn Book*, *Kirkus Reviews*, *Booklist*, and *Bulletin of the Center for Children's Books*. But these lists and journals are only a starting point. To know if a title will work, you must read it aloud several times.

Look for books with a straightforward story line that can be absorbed in one listening. A good read aloud has pleasing language and is satisfying in some way. The illustrations are a prime consideration. Can they be seen and appreciated by a group? Are the illustrations distinct and uncluttered? Do they enhance the text or distract from it? Are the illustrations appropriately placed? It's confusing and frustrating to children if you're talking about a boy who discovers a magic box, and they don't see the accompanying visual until you turn the page.

Several types of books work well with preschoolers. John Burningham's *Mr. Gumpy's Outing* is an example of a cumulative story. Each action builds on the one before to an inevitable climax. Mr. Gumpy invites numerous animals and two children for a ride in his boat. He tells each character to behave in a certain way; they don't and the boat tips over. They all swim to shore and have tea together. The book also has distinctive characters; swift plotting; and a clear beginning, middle, and end.

The Three Billy Goats Gruff, written by P. C. Asbjørnsen and illustrated by Marcia Brown, features repetition of action and language. Most folktales share this quality. The three billy goats must cross a bridge beneath which lives a mean troll. Each goat "trip traps" over the bridge, and each is threatened by the troll. The setting, characters, and conflict are established quickly, and once the climax arrives, the ending comes swiftly. Folktales are an excellent choice for story hour because they are meant to be read or told aloud.

In *The Snowy Day*, Ezra Jack Keats evokes a mood. Children can join Peter on his adventures in the city on a snowy day. The words are carefully chosen; the colors are bold and vibrant. The mood is one of joy with nature.

Children also like stories that have a character with whom they can identify. In *Happy Birthday, Sam* by Pat Hutchins, Sam thinks that a birthday means he can suddenly do things that he couldn't do before.

Also share stories that have a character who is in a situation or who exhibits an emotion with which children can identify. Check out *David and Dog* by Shirley Hughes in which David loses his beloved stuffed animal.

The story hour brings together children with different interests, tastes, and ranges of experience, so provide stories with various themes or treatments of a single theme and stories with varying plots, characters, settings, tempos, and artistic qualities. Use books that will stretch the imagination, make children curious and satisfy their curiosity, tell them something about the world in a familiar or new way, or make them laugh. Make a special effort to use well-written books with female characters in the main role. These are still difficult to find for this age group.

You'll want to share books that are well executed in terms of style, content, format, and packaging. In general then, hardcover books are preferable to paperback editions.

Never assume that children have heard the "classics," i.e., *The Three Little Pigs, Angus and the Ducks* by Marjorie Flack, or *Where the Wild Things Are* by Maurice Sendak. They might not have. And even if they have, children like to hear a good story again and again. If a story fits into several program subjects, use it more than once in different ways—as a book talk, a read aloud, or a felt board story. Share different interpretations of the same story—different retellings, different illustrations, or both.

Ultimately, the most important consideration in choosing stories to read aloud is to select stories that you like and which interest you. You can't generate enthusiasm for something you dislike.

There are many excellent books that you'll want to share with the children but either won't have time for or won't find appropriate to read aloud to a group, so do a book talk. Tell the children enough about the book to make them want to share it with someone at home. Books that fall into this category include:

- Small format books.

- Books with illustrations that are small or pale.

- Books in which the story is too long. They can be shared in two or more sittings at home.

- Nonfiction titles.

- Wordless books. Children can make up their own words and story at home.

- Books with chapters.

- Books that require a special child to appreciate them.

- Books in which the text is interrupted for several pages by illustrations.

- Books in which text also appears in the illustrations.

- Books that are different editions of stories used as read alouds.

You'll also select other material to use in your programs to provide a change of pace and to offer other experiences with language. Tell-and-draw stories are short tales that evolve on a chalkboard or a piece of paper. Fold-and-cut stories culminate in a paper creation that you cut out as you tell the rhyme, story, or song.

Many titles can be turned into felt board or flannel board stories. Look for stories that do not require a lot of characters, settings, or objects. You don't want to manipulate too many items. Stories that work well on the felt board include *Moon Bear* by Frank Asch, *Why the Sun and the Moon Live in the Sky* by Dayrell Elphinstone, *Caps for Sale* by Esphyr Slobodkina, and *The Gunniwolf* by Wilhelmina Harper. Some rhymes and songs can be turned into felt board stories too.

Choose poems that are within the children's ability to understand, with appropriate language and images. Use collections or single poems with illustrations you can show to a group. Examine poetry books written by Jack Prelutsky and those edited by Lenore Blegvad. Don't forget Mother Goose. Children like to hear poems that are familiar to them. Check out Mother Goose collections illustrated by Marguerite de Angeli, Tomie dePaola, and Brian Wildsmith. Children also like stories in verse, such as *May I Bring a Friend* by Beatrice Schenk de Regniers.

Most participation books for this age group are visual guessing games. Many clever titles are available, including Tana Hoban's *Look Again, Puzzles* by Brian Wildsmith, and *Find the Cat* by Elaine Livermore.

Children enjoy fingerplays with broad and easy actions. Counting hand rhymes are popular, and you'll find a generous selection of them. Action rhymes are also particularly successful. Children have the opportunity to move their entire bodies, not just their hands or fingers.

Children like to sing, and there are many popular tunes and folk songs you can share with them. Use songs with repetition, such as "Old MacDonald Had a Farm" and "This Old Man." Children either know the song or quickly catch on to the tune and the words. Beautifully illustrated versions of individual songs exist, and they are perfect to share with a group. You'll find a list of them in the last program plan, "Let's Make Music." Don't forget to use action songs, such as "I'm a Little Teapot," in which the children sing and do simple actions.

Creative dramatics works well too. Select rhymes, poems, short stories, or parts of stories that children can act out.

Most filmstrips for children are based on picture book stories and use the text and illustrations from the books. They vary considerably in quality, so use them selectively. Use a filmstrip version of a book when:

- The book is too small for group presentation.

- The sound track enhances the story.

- The narrator (sometimes the author of the book) gives an excellent interpretation of the story.

- There are a few textless pages in the book that are bridged with music in the filmstrip.

Some excellent films have been produced for children. With the easy accessibility of cable television, many children have seen the films available to you. But they like to see them again. Use the same criteria you would use in evaluating books to select appropriate films.

It's worth keeping track of material that you find on eight-by-five-inch file cards or in a notebook. List the program subject, and then leave ample space to enter titles for each heading: read alouds, book talks, other story forms, poetry, fingerplays and action rhymes, songs, films and filmstrips, and activities.

ORGANIZING AND ARRANGING THE MATERIAL

A program thirty to forty-five minutes long works well with four and five year olds. Be flexible, though. If the children are restless for a particular session (it's a rainy day; it's Halloween), don't use all of your material.

There are several ways to open your program. You might:

- Have a short discussion on the topic.

- Tell a one- or two-minute story.

- Do a book talk.

- Share a poem.

- Settle everyone with a fingerplay.

Place longer stories at the beginning of the program when everyone is most attentive. Use fingerplays, action rhymes, or songs as a change of pace within the program. Participation books, creative dramatics, and other activities are best shared at the end of the program. It's often difficult for children to settle down after these. Films and filmstrips work well near the end of the program, but like shorter stories, other story forms, book talks, and poetry, they can be used in whatever slot seems appropriate.

PREPARING FOR THE STORY HOUR

Don't rely on an off-the-cuff performance. Be familiar with your material. Practice the stories you intend to read aloud, and think of short comments to introduce each story.

Extemporaneous book talks are effective. Write your talk on a file card, in note form preferably, and use the card as a reference. Don't recite the entire plot. Instead, set up the dilemma, problem, or conflict in the book. Reveal enough to entice someone to bring the book home and find out "what happened next." Mark illustrations from the book that correspond to your comments. Share these illustrations when you do the book talk.

Practice fingerplays and action rhymes until you can do them easily without the book. Practice felt board stories until you can manipulate the felt pieces smoothly. The same adage applies to tell-and-draw stories and fold-and-cut stories.

You can buy a felt board or you can make one. Take a piece of wood about twenty-four by thirty inches, stretch a piece of felt over it, and then tack the felt to the board with heavy staples. Story pieces are best made out of felt.

"Preview" is the key word when using filmstrips and films. You don't want any surprises during the program. Be sure that the film or filmstrip you purchased or borrowed is the correct title. Also, check that a borrowed film does not run backward or upside down or jumpy. Be sure that the sound is audible. If you borrow a film or filmstrip and find that the colors are flat, the pacing is too slow, or it's inappropriate for four and five year olds, don't use it.

While preparing for the story hour, jot down comments that will connect each book or activity to the next item or to other items in the program. These comments will lend coherence to your material.

AGE OF CHILDREN

You'll find that you can share a greater variety of stories and activities with four and five year olds than you can with three to five year olds. If possible, hold a separate program for three year olds.

THE SERIES

A series is effective because it takes children and their parents time to get used to coming to story hour. A series of programs also gives you the chance to develop a rapport with the children. And you can develop programs ranging from those which use simple materials to those which use longer, more complex stories and activities.

You can run your program from fall through spring, in ten-week sessions, in six-week sessions — the length of the series depends on interest, your schedule, and staffing. Some programmers break during the winter months when attendance falls off due to sickness or bad weather. Other programmers begin in October because they need September to plan programs after a hectic summer schedule.

REGISTRATION

It's advisable to hold a registration period for the entire series. The registration allows you to limit the size of your group. Twenty to twenty-five preschoolers is usually the most one person can handle and still do an effective program. Take additional names on a waiting list in case anyone drops out. If demand is great, you might need two story hour sessions. You can hold the registration for several days or a week or until the maximum number of children has signed up.

Some programmers let people register over the phone. However, there are advantages to registering children in person. You can meet the children, and they can meet you; you can familiarize the children with the library if they haven't visited before; you can get the children excited about attending the program; and you can answer the parents' or the care givers' questions. You'll have the opportunity to explain the format and the purpose of the program to the adults and to orient them to library services. Also, you can take special considerations into account before the series begins. Does a child have a hearing or visual impairment? He can be seated at the front of the group.

Give the parent or the care giver a form to fill out. On the bottom of the form, ask for information including child's name, address, phone number, age, and name of parent. The rest of the form, which you give to the adult, lists information about the program. This handout also serves as a reminder about the program.

PUBLICITY

The amount and kind of publicity needed will vary. If the story hour is an established program in your community, then people will probably ask you about it. If attendance hasn't been good in past years or you're initiating story hour in your area, then you'll want to use most or all of the different types of publicity available.

Write an article for the local newspaper's community bulletin board. Be sure to include the name and a brief description of the program, age of registrants, time, day, dates, location, name of contact person, and phone number. Radio stations air announcements for nonprofit institutions. Be concise! Many local cable television stations air public-service announcements too. Contact the station for details on how it wants the information to be submitted.

If you film story hours, use some of your footage to create an ad for the cable television station's community-access channel. If you're lucky, the station will provide a volunteer to help you with your idea. Here's a storyboard for an ad:

Audio	Video
Would you like your preschooler to enjoy good books?	Children listening to story
Would you like your preschooler to enjoy fingerplays, rhymes, songs, and filmstrips?	Children doing fingerplay
Would you like your child to catch the reading habit?	Children listening to story
Then put your child in the picture.	Group of children
Sign up for picture book story hour.	Group of children
(Audio same as video)	For more information, call the Thomas Crane Public Library, 471-2400

Posters can be effective especially if they have striking visuals. You might use an illustration or a photograph of children's faces with the slogan "Put Your Child in the Picture, Sign up for Picture Book Story Hour." Include program information. Tack posters in the children's room; the adult department of the library where parents will see them; and local stores where adults and children go, i.e., grocery, shoe, and clothing stores.

Bookmarks, handouts, and flyers with program information on them can be effective too. Cut bookmarks out in interesting shapes, such as a bookworm or a rocket ship. Use interesting visuals on your handouts and flyers — a carousel or a character from a book that you'll be sharing during story hour perhaps. Don't just leave these items on a desk or table. Hand them to people. Mail flyers to local parents' cooperatives.

LOCATION AND SPACE REQUIREMENTS

A separate program room has many advantages. It can always be set up for programming, and during the program, there won't be interruptions from other library activities. If the room is very large, define a smaller area for the program so the children won't be moving all around. I solved this problem by placing my seat near a wall and putting a table of display books behind the children.

If a separate room is not available, try to find a quiet corner of the children's area. Define the program space with a rug or rug squares on which the children can sit.

Be sure the children don't face anything distracting, such as a window or a corridor. A bookcase serves as a good neutral backdrop.

Often, you don't have a choice about the amount of space available to you. If you do, try to use an area at least twelve-feet square.

YOU'RE ON — THE PROGRAM

Here are a few suggestions to consider:

Make name tags for each child. Keep them simple — a ball, a bear, a top. The tags can be attached with a safety pin or strung with a piece of yarn. Name tags are especially helpful when you're trying to learn each child's name.

If you can, sit on a low bench. A bench places you closer to the children than a chair, and it's less formal. Whether the children sit on a rug, rug squares, or cushions, try to arrange them in a semicircle so that they can all see you and the books clearly.

Before the program begins, ask the parents and the care givers to leave the program space. You should emphasize this at the registration. Children often behave differently in front of their parents. Sometimes, the adults are noisy, and you compete with them for the children's attention. Perhaps there's a room they can go to if they have younger children with them. If this isn't possible, ask them to sit away from the program space.

Preface each book with the title and the name of the author and illustrator. Hold each read aloud in one hand slightly away from and in front of your body. Panning, moving the book from side to side, isn't necessary, and it can be distracting.

In general, it's best to let the story speak for itself. Interjections can be annoying. If you ask questions about a story, be sure that you can relate the children's comments to the next activity.

When you do a book talk, show illustrations from the book that correspond to what you're talking about. When you share a filmstrip or film, try to have a copy of the accompanying book if one exists or is available.

Never force a child to participate in an activity. Let him watch and/or join at his own pace.

Discipline problems can occur even if you have excellent material and a lively presentation. Don't ignore these incidents. Address the problem immediately and firmly. If a child is talking, interject the child's name into the story. An example is " 'Timmy,' the little red hen said. . . ." Sometimes one child annoys another. Separate them and seat one of them near you. Don't let anyone spoil the group's good time.

PROGRAMS FOR PARENTS

A logical companion to the story hour is programs for the parents and care givers. Ask a librarian from the adult department to give a talk on child-care books, how-to books, cookbooks, financial management books, or any other subject you think would interest these adults.

Invite a school psychologist to talk about preparing children for the first day of school. Ask the supervisor of children's services to talk about books to use with children of various ages.

EVALUATION

It's worth taking a few minutes after each story hour to note how successful each book or activity was and if each item's placement in the program was effective. These steps will help you plan future programs.

Carnival of the
Animals
An Introductory Program

PUBLICITY

Print information pertaining to the program on bookmarks cut in the shape of a bookworm, and hand them out to parents and children when books are charged out. Use animals joined tail to trunk as the visual for posters and flyers. Create a carousel for your bulletin board. You can use pictures from magazines or draw the animals yourself. Be sure to include program information: date, time, location, and subject.

PROGRAM PLAN

So much to get used to! For some children the story hour will furnish their first experience with other young people. For others it will be the first time they must sit and listen for any length of time. A new situation, a new adult to relate to . . . so the first program should consist of short stories and several participatory activities. Use some materials with which you think the children will be familiar. Help them feel comfortable. Use a friendly animal puppet. Don't feel compelled to use all the material you have planned. Be flexible. End your program with a tour of the library's children's room. Be sure to introduce the children to other staff members with whom they might come into contact.

Fingerplay

"Ten Little Fingers," p. 36 in **Ring a Ring O' Roses: Stories, Games and Finger Plays for Pre-School Children**, rev. ed. Flint, Mich.: Flint Public Library, 1981.

Relax the children first. Draw them into the program by sharing this fingerplay with them. Preface the fingerplay by saying, "Before I tell you some stories, let's learn a story together on our hands." Slowly say the fingerplay, and do the actions suggested. Ask the children to watch and listen. Next, have the children try the words and actions with you. Share the fingerplay again.

Ten Little Fingers

(Hold up ten fingers. Suit actions to words.)

I have ten little fingers,
And they all belong to me.
I can make them do things,
Would you like to see?

I can close them up tight.
I can open them wide.
I can hold them up high.
I can hold them down low.
I can wave them to and fro,
And I can hold them just so.

Poetry

"Hey Diddle Diddle" in **Nicola Bayley's Book of Nursery Rhymes**. il. by Nicola
  Bayley. New York: Alfred A. Knopf, 1975.
  Say the rhyme with the book held up so that the children can see the illustrations. Repeat and invite the children to say the rhyme with you if they know
it. Tell the children that you'll share many rhymes with them in the weeks to
come.

Read Aloud

Curious George by H. A. Rey. il. by author. Boston: Houghton Mifflin, 1941.
  Hold up the book, and ask the children if they are familiar with Curious
George. You might continue, "George is a little monkey who likes to find out
about things. Often his curiosity gets him into trouble. Let's see what kind of
trouble George gets into."

Read Aloud

Turtle Tale by Frank Asch. il. by author. New York: Dial Press, 1978.
  Preface this story with comments such as, "Turtle is so confused. He
wears a shell, but he doesn't know when he should put his head in or stick it
out. This gets him into all sorts of trouble."
  You can use this book as the basis for a creative dramatics activity at the
end of the program. If the children were turtles, would they stick their heads in
or out if certain things happened? The children can indicate which they would
do by holding their heads in the air or hiding their heads with their hands.
Possible situations: A big wind blows. A huge hawk flies overhead. It snows.

Action Rhyme

"An elephant goes like this and that," p. 103 in **Games for the Very Young:
  Finger Plays and Nursery Games** compiled by Elizabeth Matterson. New
  York: American Heritage Press/McGraw-Hill, c1969, 1971.
  From talking about or "being" a very small animal, you are going to
become a large animal. Ask the children to watch you do this rhyme.
Demonstrate the action for the trunk several times because this is confusing to

some children. Ask the children to stand, and be sure that everyone can see you. Invite the children to do the rhyme with you. Repeat.

"An elephant goes like this and that."*

An elephant goes like this and that.
(Pat knees.)

He's terrible big,
(Put hands up high.)

And he's terrible fat.
(Put hands out wide.)

He has no fingers,
(Wriggle fingers.)

And he has no toes,
(Touch toes.)

But goodness gracious, what a nose!
(Making curling movement away from nose.)

Fingerplay

"Hands on Shoulders," p. 93 in **Story Programs: A Source Book of Materials** by Carolyn Sue Peterson and Brenny Hall. Metuchen, N.J.: Scarecrow, 1980.

This fingerplay, like the previous one, has broad actions that make it perfect for large group presentation. Do the actions slowly as you recite the rhyme. Ask the children to watch and listen. Then have the children join you. If they seem interested, repeat.

---

*From *Games for the Very Young: Finger Plays and Nursery Games* compiled by Elizabeth Matterson. Copyright © 1969, 1971 by American Heritage Press/McGraw-Hill. Used by permission.

Hands on Shoulders

(Follow action as rhyme indicates.)

Hands on shoulders, hands on knees,
Hands behind you, if you please;
Touch your shoulders, now your nose,
Now your hair and now your toes;
Hands up high in the air,
Down at your sides and touch your hair;
Hands up high as before,
Now clap your hands, one, two, three, four.

Read Aloud

Milton the Early Riser by Robert Kraus. il. by Jose Aruego and Ariane
   Aruego. New York: Windmill Books, 1972.
   Introduce the story: "Milton is a panda bear. One morning he gets up
before everyone else, and he has no one to play with. What will Milton do?"
   After the story, ask the children what they do when they get up before
everyone else.

Read Aloud

Inch by Inch by Leo Lionni. il. by author. New York: Astor-Honor, 1960.
   Introduce the story: "In this story we'll meet a small inchworm with a big
problem. A large bird wants to eat him. How will he get out of this trouble?"

Read Aloud

Animals Should Definitely Not Wear Clothing by Judith Barrett. il. by Ron
   Barrett. New York: Atheneum, 1979.
   Because the text is so brief, it is easy to rush through this story. Don't. The
children need time to savor the illustrations if you want them to appreciate the
humor of the book. Each illustration shows an animal wearing clothing in a
ludicrous manner.

Participation Book

Guess What? by Roger Bester. photos by author. New York: Crown, 1980.
   This book has concealed views of a variety of animals together with questions that give clues to their identity. Show one animal in its hidden state, and
ask the children the questions. See if they can identify the animal. Do several
of the animals if the children seem interested. Suggest that someone borrow
the book and continue the game at home.

Book Talk

Ed Emberley's ABC by Ed Emberley. il. by author. Boston: Little, Brown, 1978.

Show the cover of this alphabet book. Then show several pages complete with their many objects that begin with a certain letter. Point out some of the objects. Ask the children to name other things that begin with the letter shown.

Good-Night, Owl! by Pat Hutchins. il. by author. New York: Macmillan, 1972.

Introduce the story: "Buzz, buzz, buzz. Rat-a-tat-tat. Chirp, chirp, chirp. The woodland animals are keeping owl awake. Owl can't sleep with all that noise! Finally, the other animals go to sleep, and owl has a chance to get even with them. If you want to know what owl does, share this book with someone at home."

Love from Uncle Clyde by Nancy Winslow Parker. il. by author. New York: Dodd, Mead, 1977.

Introduce the story: "What would you do with a hippo if you got one for your birthday? That's the problem the boy in this story faces. What will he feed the hippo? How will he bathe it? And will he be able to play with it?"

TRY THIS!

Read Aloud

Ets, Marie Hall. **In the Forest**. il. by author. New York: Viking Press, 1972.

Ginsburg, Mirra. **Chick and the Duckling**. il. by Jose Aruego and Ariane Dewey. New York: Macmillan, 1972.

Ginsburg, Mirra. **Three Kittens**. il. by Giulio Maestro. New York: Crown, 1973.

Kalan, Robert. **Jump, Frog, Jump!** il. by Byron Barton. New York: Greenwillow Books, 1981.

Keats, Ezra Jack. **Over in the Meadow**. text based on the original by Olive A. Wadsworth. il. by author. New York: Four Winds Press, 1972.

Keats, Ezra Jack. **Pet Show!** il. by author. New York: Macmillan, 1972.

Kent, Jack. **The Fat Cat**. il. by author. New York: Parents Magazine Press, 1971. (Adapts into a felt board story.)

Kraus, Robert. **Owliver**. il. by Jose Aruego and Ariane Dewey. New York: Windmill Books, 1974.

Book Talk

Aruego, Jose. **Look What I Can Do**. il. by author. New York: Scribner's, 1971.

Aruego, Jose, and Ariane Dewey. **We Hide, You Seek**. il. by authors. New York: Greenwillow Books, 1979.

Other Story Forms

"Choosing a Pet," pp. 20-21 in **Tell and Draw Stories** by Margaret J. Olson. Minneapolis, Minn.: Creative Storytime Press, 1963.

Poetry

"The Handiest Nose," pp. 8-9, and "The Little Turtle," p. 10 in **A Child's First Book of Poems**. il. by Cyndy Szekeres. Racine, Wis.: Western Publishing, 1981.

Participation Book

Carle, Eric. **Do You Want to Be My Friend?** il. by author. New York: Thomas Y. Crowell, 1971.

Garten, Jan. **The Alphabet Tale**. il. by Muriel Batherman. New York: Random House, 1964.

Fingerplay and Action Rhyme

"Animals," p. 124 in **One Two Three Four: Number Rhymes and Finger Games** compiled by Mary Grice. il. by Denis Wrigley. New York: Frederick Warne, 1970.

"Animals," p. 29, and "Reach for the Ceiling," p. 35 in **Ring a Ring O' Roses: Stories, Games and Finger Plays for Pre-School Children**, rev. ed. Flint, Mich.: Flint Public Library, 1981.

"Clap Your Hands," p. 10 in **Let's Do Fingerplays** by Marion F. Grayson. il. by Nancy Weyl. Washington, D.C.: Robert B. Luce, 1962.

"Little Squirrel," p. 15 in **My Big Book of Fingerplays: A Fun-to-Say, Fun-to-Play Collection** by Daphne Hogstrom. il. by Sally Augustiny. Racine, Wis.: Western Publishing, 1974.

Song

"Over in the Meadow," pp. 85-86 in **Do Your Ears Hang Low? Fifty More Musical Fingerplays** by Tom Glazer. il. by Mila Lazarevich. Garden City, N.Y.: Doubleday, 1980.

Film

The Mole in the Zoo. New York: Phoenix Films & Video, 1974. 10 min.

Rainbow
of Colors

PUBLICITY

Decorate your bulletin board with rainbows, balloons, a box of crayons, and some colorful hats. Be sure to include program information — time, date, location, and titles of some of the books you'll be sharing — in the display. Make handouts in the shape of rainbows or crayons, or draw balloons on your handouts. If time allows, create a huge rainbow or crayon for one wall. Be sure to include program information.

PROGRAM PLAN

Wear a painter's smock and painter's cap to get in the mood for this program. You might have, or you can borrow, fabrications of balloons and crayons for the wall. Hang a real bouquet of different-colored balloons in the room.

Introduction

Show the children examples of things that come in many colors: balloons, crayons, library books, hats. . . .

Is It Red? Is It Yellow? Is It Blue? by Tana Hoban. photos by author. New York: Greenwillow Books, 1978.
This book has excellent photographs of common objects that come in many colors. Show the children some of the photos, such as of the leaves, the shoes, and the gum balls. Invite the children to talk about other things that come in many colors. Suggest that someone look at the other photographs in this book later.

Colors by John J. Reiss. il. by author. Scarsdale, N.Y.: Bradbury Press, 1969.
You can continue this introduction to colors by mentioning that for each color you are sure the children can name many objects which are that color. Show the page in this book which depicts items that are red. Ask the children to name other objects not seen on the page that are usually red. If the children seem interested, continue this game with another color in the book.

Poetry

What Is Pink? by Christina Rossetti. il. by Jose Aruego. New York: Macmillan, 1971.

Use this book to make the transition into your stories. Tell the children that the woman who wrote this poem also talks about things which come in each color — some items they might never have thought of before.

Read Aloud

Caps for Sale by Esphyr Slobodkina. il. by author. Reading, Mass.: W. R. Scott, 1947.
Introduce the story: "In this story we'll meet a man who sells different-colored caps. Let's find out how one day his caps turned into a rainbow."
This adapts well into a felt board story and can be used as a creative dramatics activity.

Read Aloud

A Rainbow of My Own by Don Freeman. il. by author. New York: Viking Press, 1966.
Introduce the story: "A little boy wishes for a rainbow to play with. But what can you do with a rainbow for a friend?"

Rhyme

"Baa Baa Black Sheep," p. 50, and "Little Boy Blue," p. 25 in **Tomie dePaola's Mother Goose**. il. by Tomie dePaola. New York: Putnam, 1985.
Tell the children that there are many rhymes with colors in them. Say the rhymes, and then ask the children to say them with you. Sing the first one, and invite the children to join you.

Fingerplay

"Make the Plum Pudding," p. 33 in **Listen! And Help Tell the Story** by Bernice Wells Carlson. il. by Burmah Burris. Nashville, Tenn.: Abingdon, 1965.
Introduce the fingerplay: "Foods come in many colors too. Here's a story about purple food."
Show the children how to do the fingerplay. Go through the individual actions with the children, and then do the fingerplay together. Do it a second time.
The actions are broad enough that you can share this fingerplay with a large group of children.

Make the Plum Pudding*

Into a big bowl put the plums	(Put plums in bowl.)
Stir-about, stir-about, stir-about, stir!	(Stir.)
Next the good white flour comes;	(Add flour.)
Stir-about, stir-about, stir-about, stir!	(Stir.)
Add sugar, and peel, eggs, and spice;	(Add new ingredients.)
Stir-about, stir-about, stir-about, stir!	(Stir.)
Mix them and fix them	(Stir again and taste.)
And cook them twice.	(Place bowl in oven.)
Then eat it up! Eat it up! Eat it up!	(Eat.)
UMMMMMMMM!	(Rub stomach.)

Read Aloud

A Color of His Own by Leo Lionni. il. by author. New York: Pantheon Books, 1975.
Introduce the story: "Why does a chameleon change colors all the time? Will he ever get his wish and finally be one color?"

Read Aloud

Little Blue and Little Yellow by Leo Lionni. il. by author. New York: Astor-Honor, 1959.
Introduce the story: "Watch what happens when these two best friends become separated from each other and then get back together."

---

*From *Listen! And Help Tell the Story* by Bernice Wells Carlson. Copyright © 1965 by Abingdon Press. Used by permission.

Flip Story

The Chalk Box Story by Don Freeman. il. by author. Philadelphia: J. B. Lippincott, 1976.

Introduce the story: "Meet eight sticks of chalk that are eager to jump out of their box and tell you a colorful story."

This is a small book, so you might want to draw each page on a large sheet of paper. Attach the sheets of paper to an easel, and flip each page back as you tell the story. An attention grabber! The book is small enough that you can hold it in your right hand and read the text as you show the corresponding picture on the easel. It's most effective, however, if you memorize the story.

Book Talk

The Big Orange Splot by Daniel Manus Pinkwater. il. by author. New York: Hastings House Publishers, 1977.

Introduce the story: "Watch what happens when a man gets a big orange blob of paint on his house. Does he wash it off? Oh, no. He decides to add other colors to his house. And he doesn't stop there."

Oh, Were They Ever Happy by Peter Spier. il. by author. Garden City, N.Y.: Doubleday, 1978.

Introduce the story: "What would happen if you decided to paint your parents' house? Would they be happy? Find out how the children in this story paint their house. It's a lot of work, very messy, but fun too. Do you think their parents will be pleased with the results?"

Participation Book

But Where Is the Green Parrot? by Thomas Zacharias. il. by author. New York: Delacorte Press, 1978.

On each page a green parrot is hidden among many colorful objects — on a table, in a train, for example. The children must find the parrot. Show each two-page spread to about five children at a time, and then ask if everyone knows where the parrot is. Let someone point to it. Be sure to point out the parrot yourself to be sure that everyone sees it.

Filmstrip

Harold and the Purple Crayon by Crockett Johnson. il. by author. Weston, Conn.: Weston Woods, n.d. 7 min.

Preface the filmstrip by showing the children a large purple crayon. Ask them if they'd like to have a purple crayon that is magical — magical enough that whatever they drew with it would become real. Tell them that Harold has a crayon like that. Invite the children to watch what Harold draws and to see what happens to Harold because of what he draws. At the end of the filmstrip, ask the children what their favorite things were that Harold drew.

TRY THIS!

Read Aloud

Brunhoff, Laurent de. **Babar's Book of Colors**. il. by author. New York: Random House, 1984.

Cohen, Miriam. **No Good in Art**. il. by Lillian Hoban. New York: Greenwillow Books, 1980.

DePaola, Tomie. **Marianna May and Nursey**. il. by author. New York: Holiday House, 1983.

Hadithi, Mwenye. **Greedy Zebra**. il. by Adrienne Kennaway. Boston: Little, Brown, 1984.

Hirsch, Marilyn. **How the World Got Its Color**. il. by author. New York: Crown, 1972.

Lobel, Arnold. **The Great Blueness and Other Predicaments**. il. by author. New York: Harper & Row, 1968.

Zion, Gene. **Harry the Dirty Dog**. il. by Margaret Bloy Graham. New York: Harper & Row, 1956.

Book Talk

Bright, Robert. **My Red Umbrella**. il. by author. New York: William Morrow, 1959.

Carrick, Malcolm. **Splodges**. il. by author. New York: Viking Press, 1975.

Charlip, Remy, and Burton Supree. **Harlequin and the Gift of Many Colors**. il. by Remy Charlip. New York: Parents Magazine Press, 1973.

Duvoisin, Roger. **The House of Four Seasons**. il. by author. New York: Lothrop, Lee & Shepard Books, 1956.

Rice, Eve. **New Blue Shoes**. il. by author. New York: Macmillan, 1975.

Testa, Fulvio. **If You Take a Paintbrush**. il. by author. New York: Dial Press, 1982.

Poetry

"My Coloring Book," pp. 40-43 in **Rainy Rainy Saturday** by Jack Prelutsky. il. by Marilyn Hafner. New York: Greenwillow Books, 1980.

O'Neill, Mary O. **Hailstones and Halibut Bones: Adventures in Color**. il. by Leonard Weisgard. Garden City, N.Y.: Doubleday, 1961.

Fingerplay and Action Rhyme

"The Rainbow," p. 32 in **Finger Frolics: Over 250 Fingerplays for Young Children from 3 Years**, rev. ed. compiled by Liz Cromwell, Dixie Hibner, and John R. Faitel. il. by Joan Lockwood. Livonia, Mich.: Partner Press, 1983.

"What Color Are You Wearing?" p. 41 in **Ring a Ring O' Roses: Stories, Games and Finger Plays for Pre-School Children**, rev. ed. Flint, Mich.: Flint Public Library, 1981.

"What Colors Do I See?" p. 45 in **Rhymes for Fingers and Flannelboards** by Louise Binder Scott and J. J. Thompson. il. by Jean Flowers. Minneapolis, Minn.: Webster Publishing/T. S. Denison, 1960.

Film

Harold and the Purple Crayon. Weston, Conn.: Weston Woods, 1969. 8 min.

Activities

"Pantomime Activity."
Introduce the activity: "What is something (name of color) we can be?" Invite the children to act out the various situations below.

Red:	Bounce a red ball. Sniff a red rose. Sound like a fire engine.
Orange:	Eat an orange. Try to catch an orange butterfly.
Yellow:	Pretend to be the sun shining. Quack like a duck. Peel and eat a banana.
Green:	Jump like a frog. Pretend to be a tree.
Blue:	Swim in the ocean. Drink a glass of water. Fly a kite in the sky. Row a boat on the water.
Brown:	Dig a garden. Pet a brown dog.

—Activity developed by Paula Gaj Sitarz

Down
on the Farm

PUBLICITY

Decorate your bulletin board with a large barn made out of construction paper. Place pictures of animals (either drawn or cut from magazines) in the windows of the barn, or create an entire farm scene. Put information about the program on the top of the barn or on a fence in front of it.

Bookmarks or handouts made in the shape of haystacks or cornstalks are easy to do. If time allows, create a scarecrow out of poster board, print information about the program on its shirt, and mount the scarecrow on a wall.

PROGRAM PLAN

Set the scene for this program by wearing bib overalls and a straw hat. Sport a corncob pipe. Place a scarecrow or haystack near the program area. Bring in any stuffed farm animals you own, and display them.

Book Talk

Baby Farm Animals. il. by Garth Williams. Racine, Wis.: Western Publishing, 1959.

The soft and warm illustrations in this book provide a good introduction to the animals that live on a farm. Share a few of the large illustrations with the children, i.e., the donkey, the chicken, and the swans. Ask the children to name other animals that live on a farm.

Read Aloud

The Little Red Hen. il. by Paul Galdone. New York: The Seabury Press, 1973.

Introduce the story: "The little red hen works very hard in and around the farmhouse. But the mouse, cat, and dog who live with her never want to help with the chores. What can the little red hen do about their laziness?"

Read Aloud

Three Ducks Went Wandering by Ron Roy. il. by Paul Galdone. New York: The Seabury Press, 1979.

Introduce the story: "There are many dangers for small animals who wander away from the farm. Will the three ducks in this story see the dangers around them when they go for a walk?"

Fingerplay

"Quack! Quack! Quack!" p. 21 in **Ring a Ring O' Roses: Stories, Games and Finger Plays for Pre-School Children**, rev. ed. Flint, Mich.: Flint Public Library, 1981.

Introduce the fingerplay: "Let's share a story on our hands about two more ducks."

Broad actions make this a perfect fingerplay to use with a large group of children. Demonstrate the fingerplay. Repeat and invite the children to join in on the refrain. Do it again, and have the children try to do all of the actions.

Quack! Quack! Quack!

Five little ducks that I once knew,
(Hold up five fingers.)

Big ones, little ones, skinny ones too,
(Pantomime sizes with hands.)

But the one little duck with the
(Hold up one finger.)

Feather on his back,
All he could do was, "Quack, Quack, Quack."
(Make quacking motions with thumb and four fingers.)

All he could do was, "Quack, Quack, Quack."
Down to the river they would go,
Waddling, waddling, to and fro,
(Make waddling motions.)

But the one little duck with the
Feather on his back,
All he could do was, "Quack, Quack, Quack."
All he could do was, "Quack, Quack, Quack."
Up from the river they would come.
Ho, Ho, Ho, Ho, Hum, Hum, Hum,
But the one little duck with the
Feather on his back,
All he could do was, "Quack, Quack, Quack."
All he could do was, "Quack, Quack, Quack."

Fingerplay

"Two Mother Pigs," p. 23 in **Ring a Ring O' Roses: Stories, Games and Finger Plays for Pre-School Children**, rev. ed. Flint, Mich.: Flint Public Library, 1981.

Introduce the fingerplay: "Pigs live on farms too. Here's a story you can learn about ten pigs."

Show the children how the fingerplay is done, and then have them try the actions with you. Repeat.

Two Mother Pigs

Two mother pigs lived in a pen.
(Hold up thumbs.)

Each had four babies, and that made ten.
(Show eight fingers and two thumbs.)

These four babies were black as night.
(Show four fingers of one hand, thumb in palm.)

These four babies were black and white.
(Show opposite four fingers, thumb in palm.)

But all eight babies loved to play,
And they rolled and rolled in the mud all day.
(Roll hands over each other.)

At night, with their mother,
They curled up in a heap.
(Make fists, palms up.)

And squealed and squealed till
They went to sleep.

Read Aloud

The Woman with the Eggs adapted by Jan Wahl. il. by Ray Cruz. New York: Crown, 1974.

Introduce the story: "Here's a lady setting off for market after her hen lays a dozen eggs. She starts daydreaming and soon imagines all the wonderful things that will happen once she sells the eggs. But what really happens on her journey?"

Read Aloud

Who Took the Farmer's Hat? by Joan L. Nodset. il. by Fritz Seibel. New
York: Harper & Row, 1963.

Introduce the story: "A brisk wind blows the farmer's hat off his head.
The farmer chases after it. But will he be able to find his hat? Will the farm
animals be able to help him? Let's find out."

Read Aloud

Buzz Buzz Buzz by Byron Barton. il. by author. New York: Macmillan, 1973.

Introduce the story: "Everything is quiet and normal on the farm until the
bee starts buzzing. Let's see all the trouble that buzz, buzz, buzz causes." (This
is a cumulative story in which the bee's buzzing sets off a chain of events.)

Book Talk

Henny Penny retold by Paul Galdone. il. by Paul Galdone. New York: The
Seabury Press, 1968.

Introduce the story: "Henny Penny is sure that the sky is falling when an
acorn hits her on the head. She must tell the king! Some friends join her on the
way—Turkey Lurkey, Goosey Loosey, Cocky Locky, and Ducky Lucky. But
the trip turns dangerous for Henny Penny and her friends when they meet
Foxy Loxy who tells them that he knows an easier and faster way to the king."

Our Animal Friends on Maple Hill Farm by Alice Provensen and Martin
Provensen. il. by authors. New York: Random House, 1974.

Introduce the story: "If you want to meet more animals who live on a
farm . . . If you'd like to see what horses, goats, cows, sheep, cats, and other
animals do all day on the farm . . . then share this book with someone at
home."

Farmer Palmer's Wagon Ride by William Steig. il. by author. New York:
Farrar, Straus and Giroux, 1974.

Introduce the story: "Farmer Palmer's trip to market is uneventful. He
sells his vegetables and buys presents for everyone back home. Ah, but the trip
home is very exciting! First, Farmer Palmer and Ebenezer, his horse, are
caught in a thunderstorm. Then a tree crashes over their cart. One accident
after another happens. How will Farmer Palmer and Ebenezer ever get home
safely?"

Filmstrip

Rosie's Walk by Pat Hutchins. il. by author. Weston, Conn.: Weston Woods,
1972.

Introduce the filmstrip: "Like the three ducks we met earlier, Rosie goes for a walk around the farm. She, too, is unaware of the dangers nearby."

Song

"Old MacDonald Had a Farm," pp. 56-57 in **Eye Winker, Tom Tinker, Chin Chopper** by Tom Glazer. il. by Ron Himler. Garden City, N.Y.: Doubleday, 1973.

Introduce the song: "It's time to share a song about a farmer and his farm animals."

Many of the children will know this song, so start right in. After each verse, sing "Old MacDonald had a _____," and let the children supply the name of an animal. Continue as long as the children seem interested.

Rarely will children not shout out the names of animals. Here are some suggestions, though, just in case: duck, pig, cow, rooster, frog, horse, bird, dog, cat, donkey, sheep, goose, and turkey.

You might also like to make the animals mentioned out of felt. Put each animal on a felt board as it is introduced during the song. The song is also found in:

Old MacDonald Had a Farm. il. by Robert Quackenbush. Philadelphia: J. B. Lippincott, 1972.

Singing Bee! A Collection of Favorite Children's Songs compiled by Jane Hart. il. by Anita Lobel. New York: Lothrop, Lee & Shepard Books, 1982, p. 118.

TRY THIS!

Read Aloud

Brown, Ruth. **The Big Sneeze**. il. by author. New York: Lothrop, Lee & Shepard Books, 1985.

D'Aulaire, Ingri, and Edgar P. D'Aulaire. **Don't Count Your Chicks**. il. by authors. Garden City, N.Y.: Doubleday, 1943.

Domanska, Janina. **Busy Monday Morning**. il. by author. New York: Greenwillow Books, 1985.

Duvoisin, Roger. **The Importance of Crocus**. il. by author. New York: Alfred A. Knopf, 1980.

Galdone, Paul, adapter. **Cat Goes Fiddle-i-fee**. il. by Paul Galdone. New York: Ticknor & Fields/Houghton Mifflin, 1985.

Hogrogian, Nonny. **One Fine Day**. il. by author. New York: Macmillan, 1971.

Hutchins, Pat. **Rosie's Walk**. il. by author. New York: Macmillan, 1968.

Nakatani, Chiyoko. **My Day on the Farm**. il. by author. New York: Thomas Y. Crowell, 1976.

Book Talk

Azarian, Mary. **A Farmer's Alphabet**. il. by author. Boston: David R. Godine Publisher, 1981.

Carrick, Donald. **Milk**. il. by author. New York: Greenwillow Books, 1985.

Dalgliesh, Alice. **The Little Wooden Farmer**. il. by Anita Lobel. New York: Macmillan, 1968.

Duvoisin, Roger. **Petunia**. il. by author. New York: Alfred A. Knopf, 1950.

McPhail, David. **Farm Morning**. il. by author. New York: Harcourt Brace Jovanovich, 1985.

Noble, Trinka Hakes. **The Day Jimmy's Boa Ate the Wash**. il. by Steven Kellogg. New York: Dial Press, 1980.

Paul, Jan S. **Hortense**. il. by Madelaine Gill Linden. New York: Thomas Y. Crowell, 1984.

Provensen, Alice, and Martin Provensen. **The Year at Maple Hill Farm**. il. by authors. New York: Atheneum, 1978.

Tresselt, Alvin. **Wake up, Farm!** il. by Roger Duvoisin. New York: Lothrop, Lee & Shepard Books, 1955.

Other Story Forms

"Hickety, pickety, my black hen," p. 307 in **Handbook for Storytellers** by Caroline Feller Bauer. Chicago: American Library Association, 1977. (This is a fold-and-cut story.)

"Hortense the Chicken," pp. 24-25 in **Tell and Draw Stories** by Margaret J. Olson. Minneapolis, Minn.: Creative Storytime Press, 1963.

Poetry

"The Chickens," p. 38, and "The Barnyard," p. 39 by Maud Burnham in **A Child's First Book of Poems**. il. by Cyndy Szekeres. Racine, Wis.: Western Publishing, 1981.

Fingerplay and Action Rhyme

"Farmer and His Seeds," "Five Little Farmers," and "Five Little Pigs," p. 17 in **Ring a Ring O' Roses: Stories, Games and Finger Plays for Pre-School Children**, rev. ed. Flint, Mich.: Flint Public Library, 1981.

"One, Two, Three," p. 4 in **My Big Book of Fingerplays: A Fun-to-Say, Fun-to-Play Collection** by Daphne Hogstrom. il. by Sally Augustiny. Racine, Wis.: Western Publishing, 1974.

"Ten Little Ducklings," p. 27, "Ten Fluffy Chickens," p. 30, "Ten Little Farmer Boys," p. 37, and "Little Boy Blue," p. 106 in **Rhymes for Fingers and Flannelboards** by Louise Binder Scott and J. J. Thompson. il. by Jean Flowers. Minneapolis, Minn.: Webster Publishing/T. S. Denison, 1960.

Song

"Bingo," p. 82 in **Singing Bee! A Collection of Favorite Children's Songs** compiled by Jane Hart. il. by Anita Lobel. New York: Lothrop, Lee & Shepard Books, 1982.

"The Farmer in the Dell," p. 180 in **The Fireside Book of Children's Songs** collected and edited by Marie Winn. musical arrangements by Allan Miller. il. by John Alcorn. New York: Simon & Schuster, 1966.

Filmstrip

Charlie Needs a Cloak by Tomie dePaola. il. by author. Weston, Conn.: Weston Woods, 1977. 6 min.

Little Red Hen. il. by Paul Galdone. Old Greenwich, Conn.: Listening Library, n.d. 8 min.

Film

Rosie's Walk. Weston, Conn.: Weston Woods, 1970. 5 min.

Activities

"Animal Memory Game."

Cut out pictures of animals from old magazines. Mount the pictures on poster board, and then back them with felt. During this activity, put a few of the animals on a felt board. Cover the pictures with a piece of poster board or cloth. Wait several seconds. Ask the children to recall what they saw. Do this several times using different animals.

—Activity developed by Paula Gaj Sitarz

Goblins
and Ghosts
Halloween Stories

PUBLICITY

Orange construction paper cut out in the shape of a pumpkin and white paper cut out in the shape of a ghost are perfect for handouts or bookmarks. Your bulletin board can become a large field with an owl perched on a fence, a ghost flying through the trees, and a full moon rising in the sky. Print information about the program on the paper moon. Make posters to advertise the program. Cut out poster board in the shape of an owl, or draw a large witch on poster board, and place information about the program on her skirt.

You might want to invite the children to come to the program in costume. This is also a program you might want to open to other groups of preschoolers.

PROGRAM PLAN

Decorate the program area with a haystack, scarecrow, or pumpkins. Outfit yourself as a witch, as Mother Goose, or as a character from a book you've shared with the children. It's also easy to make a costume out of poster board. Wear it like a sandwich board. Orange poster board becomes a pumpkin costume, red becomes a tomato, and black poster board cut round with a yellow center made of construction paper becomes a record.

Poetry

"It's Halloween," pp. 7-9, "Pumpkin," pp. 18-21, and "Ghost," pp. 51-53 in
It's Halloween by Jack Prelutsky. il. by Marilyn Hafner. New York: Greenwillow Books, 1977.

A perfect book to introduce the subject! Read the three amusing selections, and then ask the children what else Halloween makes them think of. Show the light and humorous illustrations as you share the poems with the children.

Read Aloud

Miss Nelson Is Missing by James Marshall. il. by Harry Allard. Boston: Houghton Mifflin, 1977.

Introduce the story: "The kids in Room 207 are awful to their sweet teacher Miss Nelson. But one day Miss Nelson disappears. In her place comes Miss Viola Swamp. Wait until you see her! I wonder if she can make the kids behave? Listen and find out." (Miss Viola Swamp looks like a witch but is really Miss Nelson in disguise.)

Read Aloud

The Monster and the Tailor: A Ghost Story by Paul Galdone. il. by author.
New York: Ticknor & Fields/Houghton Mifflin, 1982.

Introduce the story: "The tailor is commanded by the Grand Duke to sew
a pair of lucky pants for him in the cemetery. The tailor doesn't mind doing
this until he gets to the cemetery and finds out who's hiding there."

Fingerplay

"Five Little Pumpkins," p. 58 in **Ring a Ring O' Roses: Stories, Games and
Finger Plays for Pre-School Children**, rev. ed. Flint, Mich.: Flint Public
Library, 1981.

Introduce the fingerplay: "Halloween is witches, monsters, ghosts . . . and
pumpkins too. Let's share a story on our hands about five pumpkins."

Demonstrate the fingerplay, and then invite the children to do it with you.
Repeat. Like other counting hand rhymes, this one is done while seated. It can
be used with any size group.

Five Little Pumpkins

(Hold up five fingers, and bend them down one at a time as
    verse progresses.)

Five little pumpkins sitting on a gate;
The first one said, "My, it's getting late."
The second one said, "There are witches in the air."
The third one said, "But we don't care."
The fourth one said, "Let's run, let's run."
The fifth one said, "It's Halloween fun."
"WOOOOOOOO" went the wind,
(Sway hand through air.)

And out went the lights.
(Make loud clap.)

These five little pumpkins ran fast out of sight.
(Place hands behind back.)

Felt Board Story

Humbug Witch by Lorna Balian. il. by author. Nashville, Tenn.: Abingdon,
1965.

Introduce the story: "This is the story of a little witch who can never make a spell work. Let's find out why." (The surprise is that she's really a little girl in costume.)

It's easy to do this story on the felt board if you practice it several times before the program date. The presentation is most effective if you learn the story. If time is short, type the text, and place it on your lap so that you can refer to it.

You'll need to cut the following items out of felt: a witch with removable shoes, skirt, shawl, shirt, and mask with long red hair attached; a broom; a stool; a pot; and a cat. Make the hair out of yarn. Other details in the story can be left to the children's imaginations.

Read Aloud

One Dark Night by Edna Mitchell Preston. il. by Kurt Werth. New York: Viking Press, 1969.

Introduce the story: "Let's meet some trick or treaters who are eager to scare people on Halloween night." (Instead, something scares them.)

Book Talk

Funnybones by Janet Ahlberg and Allan Ahlberg. il. by authors. New York: Greenwillow Books, 1980.

Introduce the story: "What do skeletons do when they get bored and want to get up to some mischief? They go out to scare someone. But what do they do if everyone is home asleep? That's the problem the big skeleton, the little skeleton, and the dog skeleton share."

A Woggle of Witches by Adrienne Adams. il. by author. New York: Scribner's, 1971.

Introduce the story: "It's Halloween night and time for the witches to have some fun and to do some scaring. They make their witches' brew and fly around the moon. But when they fly down to earth to do their scaring, something frightens them instead. What could be scary to a group of witches?"

That Terrible Halloween Night by James Stevenson. il. by author. New York: Greenwillow Books, 1980.

Introduce the story: "It's Halloween! Mary Ann and Louis try to scare grandpa. But grandpa doesn't scare so easily because of the horrible and terrifying Halloween night he had when he was a young boy. What happened to him? I'll give you a hint. It involved a huge pumpkin, a floor made of frogs, and an awful creature."

Hester by Byron Barton. il. by author. New York: Greenwillow Books, 1975.

Introduce the story: "What kind of Halloween will Hester the alligator have when a witch invites Hester into her home? It's sure to be exciting when the witch invites Hester to go for a ride on her broom."

Film

The Mole as a Painter. New York: Phoenix Films & Video, 1974. 11 min.

Introduce the film: "The nasty fox is scaring all the forest animals. But mole has a solution that just might take care of the fox. When mole gets done with his plan, all the animals will look like they're ready for Halloween. Watch!"

Activities

"Pass the Pumpkin." Developed by the staff of the Thomas Crane Public
Library, Quincy, Mass.

You need a small pumpkin, a real one or a knitted one, and Halloween music playing on a record player or on a cassette. Have the children sit close together in a circle. Invite them to pass the pumpkin until the music stops. The person holding the pumpkin when the music stops is a ghost. Continue as long as there is interest or until everyone is a ghost. You can use this activity with up to twenty-five children.

Alternatives: Get a large plastic pumpkin. Fill the pumpkin with small bags of goodies, one for each child in the program. Goodies can include small boxes of raisins, balloons, and bookmarks. Cover the opening of the pumpkin. Have the children pass this pumpkin. At the end of the activity, give a bag of goodies to each child.

You can also play pass the broom. Instead of passing a pumpkin, the children pass a small broom that you've fashioned out of construction paper.

For Halloween music, you might like to use the record *Songs about Halloween*. Great Neck, N.Y.: Classroom Materials, 1973.

TRY THIS!

Read Aloud

Brown, Marc. **Arthur's Halloween**. il. by author. Boston: Little, Brown, 1982.

Brown, Ruth. **A Dark, Dark Tale**. il. by author. New York: Dial Press, 1981.

Carlson, Natalie Savage. **Spooky and the Ghost Cat**. il. by Andrew Glass. New York: Lothrop, Lee & Shepard Books, 1985.

Galdone, Paul. **The Teeny Tiny Woman: A Ghost Story**. il. by author. New York: Clarion Books, 1984.

Johnston, Tony. **The Witch's Hat**. il. by Margot Tomes. New York: Putnam, 1984.

Kroll, Steven. **The Biggest Pumpkin Ever**. il. by Jean Bassett. New York: Holiday House, 1984.

Riley, James W. **The Gobble-Uns'll Git You Ef You Don't Watch Out!** il. by Joel Schick. Philadelphia: J. B. Lippincott, 1975.

Rose, David. **It Hardly Seems Like Halloween**. il. by author. New York: Lothrop, Lee & Shepard Books, 1983.

Sendak, Maurice. **Where the Wild Things Are**. il. by author. New York: Harper & Row, 1963.

Seuling, Barbara, reteller. **The Teeny Tiny Woman: An Old English Ghost Tale**. il. by Barbara Seuling. New York: Viking Press, 1976.

Stevenson, James. **What's under My Bed?** il. by author. New York: Greenwillow Books, 1983.

Book Talk

Adams, Adrienne. **Halloween Happening**. il. by author. New York: Scribner's, 1981.

Anderson, Lonzo. **The Halloween Party**. il. by Adrienne Adams. New York: Scribner's, 1974.

Bright, Robert. **Georgie**. il. by author. Garden City, N.Y.: Doubleday, 1944. (There are many titles in this series.)

Degen, Bruce. **Aunt Possum and the Pumpkin Man**. New York: Harper & Row, 1977. (This is a wordless book.)

Freeman, Don. **Tilly Witch**. il. by author. New York: Viking Press, 1969.

Gibbons, Gail. **Halloween**. il. by author. New York: Holiday House, 1984. (This is a nonfiction title.)

Johnston, Tony. **The Vanishing Pumpkin**. il. by Tomie dePaola. New York: Putnam, 1983.

Keats, Ezra Jack. **The Trip**. il. by author. New York: Greenwillow Books, 1978.

Schweninger, Ann. **Halloween Surprises**. il. by author. New York: Viking Penguin, 1984.

Vigna, Judith. **Everyone Goes as a Pumpkin**. il. by author. Chicago: Albert Whitman, 1977.

Viorst, Judith. **My Mama Says There Aren't Any Zombies, Ghosts, Vampires, Creatures, Demons, Monsters, Fiends, Goblins or Things**. il. by Kay Chorao. New York: Atheneum, 1973.

Other Story Forms

Withers, Carl. **The Tale of the Black Cat**. il. by Alan Cober. New York: Holt, Rinehart and Winston, 1966. (This is a tell-and-draw story.)

Fingerplay and Action Rhyme

"The Five Black Cats and the Witch," p. 27 in **Listen! And Help Tell the Story** by Bernice Wells Carlson. il. by Burmah Burris. Nashville, Tenn.: Abingdon, 1965.

"Five Little Goblins," "Halloween," and "Halloween Is Here," p. 58, "Pumpkin" and "Ten Little Goblins," p. 60 in **Ring a Ring O' Roses: Stories, Games and Finger Plays for Pre-School Children**, rev. ed. Flint, Mich.: Flint Public Library, 1981.

"Five Little Jack-O-Laterns" and "Once There Was a Pumpkin," p. 61 in **Finger Frolics: Over 250 Fingerplays for Young Children from 3 Years**, rev. ed. compiled by Liz Cromwell, Dixie Hibner, and John R. Faitel. il. by Joan Lockwood. Livonia, Mich.: Partner Press, 1983.

"Halloween Witches" and "Jack-O-Lanterns," p. 95, "The Friendly Ghost" and "Scary Eyes," p. 97 in **Let's Do Fingerplays** by Marion F. Grayson. il. by Nancy Weyl. Washington, D.C.: Robert B. Luce, 1962.

"Jack-O-Lantern," p. 10, and "Five Little Goblins," p. 12 in **Hand Rhymes** collected by Marc Brown. New York: E. P. Dutton, 1985.

"Ten Little Pumpkins," p. 60 in **Rhymes for Fingers and Flannelboards** by Louise Binder Scott and J. J. Thompson. il. by Jean Flowers. Minneapolis, Minn.: Webster Publishing/T. S. Denison, 1960.

Song

"The Scary Song," p. 171 in **The Fireside Book of Fun and Game Songs** collected and edited by Marie Winn. musical arrangements by Allan Miller. il. by Whitney Darrow, Jr. New York: Simon & Schuster, 1974.

"Witches Brew," p. 124 in **Hap Palmer Favorites: Songs for Learning through Music and Movement** edited by Ronny S. Schiff. songs and activities by Hap Palmer. il. by Malinda Cowles. Sherman Oaks, Calif.: Alfred Publishing, 1981.

Filmstrip

The Judge by Harve Zemach. il. by Margot Zemach. New York: Miller-Brody Productions, 1975. 5 min.

Where the Wild Things Are by Maurice Sendak. il. by author. Weston, Conn.: Weston Woods, n.d. 4 min. 30 sec.

Film

Miss Nelson Is Missing. New York: Learning Corporation of America, 1979. 14 min.

Activities

"The Dark House," p. 11 in **Juba This and Juba That: Story Hour Stretches for Large or Small Groups** selected by Virginia A. Tashjian. il. by Victoria deLarrea. Boston: Little, Brown, 1969. (This is a chant that the children repeat after the leader. It has a surprise ending.)

Here Kitty!

PUBLICITY

Decorate your bulletin board with a cat that is playing with a ball of yarn, or cover your bulletin board with cat paw prints. You can also use cat paw prints as the visual for your handouts and any posters you make to advertise the program.

PROGRAM PLAN

Introduction

Begin the program with a general chat about cats. Do any of the children own cats? What do their cats look like? How do their cats behave?

Make the transition to your program material with comments such as these: "Cats come in all shapes and sizes. Some cats are smart, some are slow. Cats can be silly, fast, large, small, quiet, noisy, or cuddly. Cats are all around us in real life, and they're found in books too."

Read Aloud

Puss in Boots by Paul Galdone. il. by author. New York: The Seabury Press, 1976.

Introduce the story: "When the miller dies, he leaves his youngest son with nothing but a cat. Ah, but this is no ordinary cat. Puss can speak, and he's bright in other ways too. He goes about the countryside using his cleverness against the king and against a giant to make things better for his master."

Read Aloud

Great Cat by David McPhail. il. by author. New York: E. P. Dutton, 1982.

Introduce the story: "Meet the biggest cat that ever lived. All the grown-ups are afraid that because he's so big Great Cat will hurt the children. But what really happens?"

Fingerplay

"Five Little Kittens," p. 64 in **Let's Do Fingerplays** by Marion F. Grayson. il. by Nancy Weyl. Washington, D.C.: Robert B. Luce, 1962.

Introduce the fingerplay: "Let's share a story on our hands about some smaller cats—five kittens."

Use this fingerplay with any number of children. Take it slowly, and do it twice before asking the children to join you. Repeat the fingerplay two or three times, so the children will have the opportunity to master the actions and some, if not all, of the words.

Five Little Kittens*

Five little kittens standing in a row,
(Extend left fingers upward, palm out.)

They nod their heads to the children, so.
(Bend fingers forward.)

They run to the left, they run to the right,
(Wiggle fingers to left, then to right.)

They stand up and stretch in the bright sunlight.
(Stretch fingers slowly.)

Along comes a dog, who's in for some fun,
(Move right fist slowly toward stretching fingers.)

M-e-o-w, see those kittens run.
(Run left fingers behind back.)

Read Aloud

The Fat Cat: A Danish Folktale by Jack Kent. il. by author. New York: Parents Magazine Press, 1971.
Introduce the story: "What happens when a small but hungry cat is left home alone with a pot of porridge?" (This is a cumulative tale in which the cat eats the pot, the porridge, and a number of people until he's stopped by a woodcutter.)

Read Aloud

Dandelion by Don Freeman. il. by author. New York: Viking Press, 1964.
Introduce the story: "Dandelion is a large cat—a lion—and he's been invited to a party at Miss Giraffe's house. He's so excited! But the day doesn't turn out the way Dandelion expected."

---

*From *Let's Do Fingerplays* by Marion F. Grayson. Copyright © 1962 by Robert B. Luce. Used by permission.

Book Talk

Millions of Cats by Wanda Gag. il. by author. New York: Coward, McCann
    & Geoghegan, 1928.
    Introduce the story: "You'll meet two lonely people in this story, a man
and a woman. They decide that a cat is just what they need to fill their home,
so the man goes in search of a cat. But what does he find? He not only finds
one cat but trillions of cats covering a mountainside. How will the man decide
which cat to take home?"

Seen Any Cats? by Frank Modell. il. by author. New York: Greenwillow
    Books, 1979.
    Introduce the story: "Milton and Marvin have a great plan. They're going
to look for cats to use in an animal act in their circus. With the money they
make from their circus, they'll be able to afford to go to the *real* circus. There's
only one catch. Will Milton and Marvin be able to train the cats they find?"

Find the Cat by Elaine Livermore. il. by author. Boston: Houghton Mifflin,
    1973.
    Introduce the story: "There's trouble brewing in this book. The dog and
the cat want the same bone, and while the dog is asleep, the cat takes the bone.
Now the dog must find the cat. Do you see the cat? If you take this book
home, you can search for the cat on every page."

TRY THIS!

Read Aloud

Brandenberg, Franz. **Aunt Nina's Visit**. il. by Aliki. New York: Greenwillow
    Books, 1984.

Calhoun, Mary. **Cross-Country Cat**. il. by Erick Ingraham. New York:
    William Morrow, 1979.

Calhoun, Mary. **Hot-Air Henry**. il. by Erick Ingraham. New York: William
    Morrow, 1981.

De Regniers, Beatrice Schenk. **So Many Cats!** il. by Ellen Weiss. New York:
    Clarion Books, 1985.

Flack, Marjorie. **Angus and the Cat**. il. by author. Garden City, N.Y.:
    Doubleday, 1931.

Gantos, Jack. **Rotten Ralph**. il. by Nicole Rubel. Boston: Houghton Mifflin, 1976.

Keats, Ezra Jack. **Pet Show!** il. by author. New York: Macmillan, 1972.

Book Talk

Kahl, Virginia. **Whose Cat Is That?** il. by author. New York: Scribner's, 1979.

Keats, Ezra Jack. **Hi, Cat!** il. by author. New York: Macmillan, 1970.

Kellogg, Steven. **A Rose for Pinkerton**. il. by author. New York: Dial Press, 1981.

Krahn, Fernando. **Catch That Cat!** il. by author. New York: E. P. Dutton, 1978. (This is a wordless book.)

Lewin, Betsy. **Cat Count**. il. by author. New York: Dodd, Mead, 1981.

Other Story Forms

"Fat Cat and Skinny Winnie," pp. 19-21 in **Lots More Tell and Draw Stories** by Margaret J. Olson. Minneapolis, Minn.: Arts & Crafts Unlimited, 1973.

"Pickles Pussy Cat," pp. 5-8 in **More Tell and Draw Stories** by Margaret J. Olson. Minneapolis, Minn.: Arts & Crafts Unlimited, 1969.

"Poor Puss," pp. 39-40 in **Tell and Draw Stories** by Margaret J. Olson. Minneapolis, Minn.: Creative Storytime Press, 1963.

Poetry

Blegvad, Lenore, ed. **Mittens for Kittens and Other Rhymes about Cats**. il. by Erik Blegvad. New York: Atheneum, 1974. (This is a collection of twenty-five poems about cats.)

"Cats," p. 40 by Eleanor Farjeon in **A Child's First Book of Poems**. il. by Cyndy Szekeres. Racine, Wis.: Western Publishing, 1981.

Fingerplay and Action Rhyme

"Counting Kittens," p. 30, "Little Kittens" and "Five Little Pussy Cats," p. 31, and "One Little Kitten, One," p. 32 in **Rhymes for Fingers and Flannelboards** by Louise Binder Scott and J. J. Thompson. il. by Jean Flowers. Minneapolis, Minn.: Webster Publishing/T. S. Denison, 1960.

"Kittens," pp. 24-25 in **Hand Rhymes** collected by Marc Brown. il. by author. New York: E. P. Dutton, 1985.

"The Puppy and the Kitty Cat," p. 36 in **Listen! And Help Tell the Story** by Bernice Wells Carlson. il. by Burmah Burris. Nashville, Tenn.: Abingdon, 1965.

Song

"I Love Little Pussy," p. 46, and "Pussy Cat, Pussy Cat," p. 50 in **Singing Bee! A Collection of Favorite Children's Songs** compiled by Jane Hart. il. by Anita Lobel. New York: Lothrop, Lee & Shepard Books, 1982.

Filmstrip

Hi, Cat! by Ezra Jack Keats. il. by author. New York: Macmillan Library Services, 1974. 3 min. 30 sec.

Pet Show! by Ezra Jack Keats. il. by author. New York: Macmillan Library Services, 1974. 4 min. 35 sec.

Teddy Bear,
Teddy Bear

PUBLICITY

Use a honey jar as the visual for your posters and handouts. Fashion a bear out of felt for your bulletin board. He can be reading a book, leaning against alphabet blocks, eating a pie, or sticking his paw in a honey jar. Invite the children to bring their favorite teddy bears to the program.

PROGRAM PLAN

Display an old-fashioned honey jar and your favorite teddy bear.

Fingerplay

"Ten Little Fingers," p. 36 in **Ring a Ring O' Roses: Stories, Games and Finger Plays for Pre-School Children**, rev. ed. Flint, Mich.: Flint Public Library, 1981.

The first story is long, so get everyone settled and listening with this fingerplay. If you used it during your first program, have the children join you immediately rather than demonstrating it first. Repeat. (Text of fingerplay is found in "Carnival of the Animals: An Introductory Program.")

Read Aloud

The Little Girl and the Big Bear retold by Joanna Galdone. il. by Paul Galdone. Boston: Houghton Mifflin, 1980.

Introduce the story: "Like all other animals, there are good bears, not very nice bears, silly bears, and selfish bears. We're going to meet one of these types of bears in our first story. Our tale begins with a little girl losing her way in the woods while picking berries. It's almost dark when the little girl finds a small house. The hut looks empty, but is it?"

Fingerplay-Song

"The Bear Went over the Mountain," p. 34 in **Let's Do Fingerplays** by Marion F. Grayson. il. by Nancy Weyl. Washington, D.C.: Robert B. Luce, 1962.

Introduce the fingerplay-song: "Why does the bear go over the mountain? Let's sing this song and find out."

You can sing or say this fingerplay depending on what you feel comfortable doing. This activity has few and easy motions. Do it once through, and then invite the children to join you. This is done while seated and can be used with a large group. The song is in:

Eye Winker, Tom Tinker, Chin Chopper by Tom Glazer. il. by Ron Himler. Garden City, N.Y.: Doubleday, 1973, p. 12.

The Bear Went over the Mountain*

The bear went over the mountain,
(Extend forearm, close and drop fist.)

The bear went over the mountain,
(Slowly creep fingers of other hand over first hand to wrist.)

The bear went over the mountain,
To see what he could see.
(Hold above position.)

And what do you think he saw?
And what do you think he saw?

The other side of the mountain,
The other side of the mountain,
The other side of the mountain,
Is all that he did see!

So the bear went down the mountain,
(Creep fingers down sloping forearm.)

So the bear went down the mountain,
So the bear went down the mountain,
Very hap-pi-ly.

Read Aloud

Corduroy by Don Freeman. il. by author. New York: Viking Press, 1968.
 Introduce the story: "Corduroy is a toy bear who lives in a department store. He's unhappy because no one will buy him. Corduroy is sure it's because he's missing a button on his overalls. What can Corduroy do about his missing button? Let's find out."

---

*From *Let's Do Fingerplays* by Marion F. Grayson. Copyright © 1962 by Robert B. Luce. Used by permission.

Book Talk

A Pocket for Corduroy by Don Freeman. il. by author. New York: Viking
   Press, 1978.
   Corduroy has more adventures when he realizes that he doesn't have a
pocket on his overalls. He trys to find a pocket and ends up in a laundry bag,
in an avalanche of snowflakes, and far away from his friend Lisa.

Action Rhyme-Song

"Teddy Bear," p. 83 in **Ring a Ring O' Roses: Stories, Games and Finger Plays
   for Pre-School Children**, rev. ed. Flint, Mich.: Flint Public Library, 1981.
   Introduce the rhyme-song: "We've been sharing stories about many types
of bears. Now it's time for us to become bears."
   This action rhyme works well with twenty to twenty-five children. Show
the children the movements. Then do the rhyme with them. Have the children
stand for "Teddy Bear." Be sure each child has enough room so that she won't
bump into her neighbor when turning. The children will catch on quickly and
will enjoy doing the rhyme again. The song is in:

Story Programs: A Source Book of Materials by Carolyn Sue Peterson and
   Brenny Hall. Metuchen, N.J.: Scarecrow, 1980, pp. 101-2.

Teddy Bear

(Standing in place, suit actions to words.)

Teddy bear, teddy bear,
Turn around;
Teddy bear, teddy bear,
Touch the ground.
Teddy bear, teddy bear,
Show your shoe;
Teddy bear, teddy bear,
That will do.

Teddy bear, teddy bear,
Go upstairs;
Teddy bear, teddy bear,
Say your prayers;
Teddy bear, teddy bear,
Turn out the light;
Teddy bear, teddy bear,
Say, "Good-night!"

Felt Board Story

Moon Bear by Frank Asch. il. by author. New York: Scribner's, 1978.

Introduce the story: "Moon bear watches the moon grow smaller and smaller. He's sure that the moon is hungry, and he decides to do something about it."

This story works well as a felt board story or as a read aloud. For the felt board version, you need the moon in all its phases, a thin moon bear, a fat moon bear, birds, glasses for bear, a house, a broom, a bowl, and a honey pot. Practice the story several times before you present it, so you can move all the felt pieces smoothly and without hesitation.

Book Talk

The Three Bears retold by Paul Galdone. il. by author. New York: The Seabury Press, 1972.

Introduce the story: "What happens when a little girl named Goldilocks breaks into the home of the three bears? Does she find anything good or interesting inside? Do the bears find her?"

This is a good read aloud too. The large illustrations work wonderfully with large groups.

Good as New by Barbara Douglass. il. by Patience Brewster. New York: Lothrop, Lee & Shepard Books, 1982.

Introduce the story: "Grady is very upset. His younger cousin K.C. just grabbed his teddy bear. K.C. treats Grady's bear terribly. He drags the teddy bear around by the ears, he tries to feed the bear to the dogs, he soaks the bear, and he buries it. Now how will Grady's bear ever be the same again?"

Bearymore by Don Freeman. il. by author. New York: Viking Press, 1976.

Introduce the story: "Poor Bearymore! The circus manager told him to think of a new circus act. But Bearymore has to sleep all winter. When will he have time to think of a new act?"

Bear's Toothache by David McPhail. il. by author. Boston: Little, Brown, 1972.

Introduce the story: "A young boy hears a bear howling in pain outside his bedroom window. The bear has a toothache! What can the little boy do to help the huge bear? And what happens if the boy's parents wake up and see the bear?"

Action Rhyme

"Let's Go on a Bear Hunt," p. 11 in **Ring a Ring O' Roses: Stories, Games and Finger Plays for Pre-School Children**, rev. ed. Flint, Mich.: Flint Public Library, 1981.

If you have a lot of room, you can do this activity with a large group. If space is limited, keep it to about twenty children. The children sit with their legs straight out. The children repeat the rhyme after you and copy your actions, so there is no need to recite this first. You also want to retain the element of surprise at the end when the children are confronted by the bear in a cave.

Save this activity for the end of the program because everyone gets very excited during this action rhyme. Usually, the children are eager to do this activity again. The rhyme is also in:

I'm Going on a Bear Hunt by Sandra Stroner Sivulich. il. by Glen Rounds. New York: E. P. Dutton, 1973.

Let's Go on a Bear Hunt

(The children repeat each line after leader.)

Let's go on a bear hunt.
(Tap hands on thighs like walking.)

All right.
Let's go.
Oh lookie.
I see a wheat field!
Can't go around it,
Can't go under it.
Let's go through it.

All right.
Let's go.
Swish, swish, swish.
(Rub hands together, like swishing through the wheat.)

Oh lookie,
I see a tree!
Can't go over it,
Can't go under it.
Let's go up it.
(Pretend to climb a tree. When top is reached, place hand on
    forehead and look around. Climb down.)

All right.
Let's go.

Oh lookie,
I see a swamp!
Can't go around it,
Can't go under it.
Let's swim through it.
(Pretend to swim.)

All right.
Let's go.

Oh lookie,
I see a bridge!
Can't go around it,
Can't go under it.
Let's cross over it.
(Make clicking sound with tongue, and stamp feet.)

All right.
Let's go.

Oh lookie,
I see a cave!
Can't go around it,
Can't go under it.
Let's go in it.
(Cup hands, and make hollow sound when clapping
     together.)

All right.
Let's go.

Golly — it's dark in here.
(Say this with suspense in voice.)

Better use my flashlight.
Doesn't work.
I think — I see something.
It's big!

It's furry!
It's got a big nose!
I think—it's a bear!
IT IS A BEAR!
LET'S GO!

(Repeat everything backwards and fast. Wipe brow, and
make a big sigh of relief.)

"WHEW! WE MADE IT!"

TRY THIS!

Read Aloud

Asch, Frank. **Bear Shadow**. il. by author. Englewood Cliffs, N.J.: Prentice-Hall, 1985.

Asch, Frank. **Bear's Bargain**. il. by author. Englewood Cliffs, N.J.: Prentice-Hall, 1985.

Asch, Frank. **Mooncake**. il. by author. Englewood Cliffs, N.J.: Prentice-Hall, 1983.

Asch, Frank. **Moongame**. il. by author. Englewood Cliffs, N.J.: Prentice-Hall, 1984.

Asch, Frank. **Skyfire**. il. by author. Englewood Cliffs, N.J.: Prentice-Hall, 1984.

Flack, Marjorie. **Ask Mr. Bear**. il. by author. New York: Macmillan, 1932.

Gage, Wilson. **Cully Cully and the Bear**. il. by author. New York: Greenwillow Books, 1983.

Ginsburg, Mirra. **Two Greedy Bears: Adapted from a Hungarian Folk Tale**. il. by Jose Aruego and Ariane Dewey. New York: Macmillan, 1976.

Gretz, Susanna. **Teddy Bears Cure a Cold**. il. by Alison Sage. New York: Four Winds Press, 1984.

Lapp, Eleanor. **The Blueberry Bears**. il. by Margot Apple. Chicago: Albert Whitman, 1983.

Lemieux, Michèle. **What's That Noise?** il. by author. New York: William Morrow, 1985.

Mack, Stan. **10 Bears in My Bed: A Goodnight Countdown**. il. by author. New York: Pantheon Books, 1974.

Murphy, Jill. **Peace at Last**. il. by author. New York: Dial Press, 1980.

Nakatani, Chiyoko. **My Teddy Bear**. il. by author. New York: Thomas Y. Crowell, 1976.

Wildsmith, Brian. **The Lazy Bear**. il. by author. New York: Franklin Watts, 1974.

Book Talk

Alexander, Martha. **Blackboard Bear**. il. by author. New York: Dial Press, 1969.

Craft, Ruth. **Winter Bear**. il. by Erik Blegvad. New York: Atheneum, 1975.

Freeman, Don. **Beady Bear**. il. by author. New York: Viking Press, 1954.

Hague, Kathleen. **Alphabears: An ABC Book**. il. by Michael Hague. New York: Holt, Rinehart and Winston, 1984.

McCloskey, Robert. **Blueberries for Sal**. il. by author. New York: Viking Press, 1948.

McLeod, Emilie W. **The Bear's Bicycle**. il. by David McPhail. Boston: Little, Brown, 1975.

McPhail, David. **Emma's Pet**. il. by author. New York: E. P. Dutton, 1985.

Turkle, Brinton. **Deep in the Forest**. il. by author. New York: E. P. Dutton, 1976. (This is a wordless book.)

Fingerplay and Action Rhyme

"Bears Everywhere," p. 53 in **Ring a Ring O' Roses: Stories, Games and Finger Plays for Pre-School Children**, rev. ed. Flint, Mich.: Flint Public Library, 1981.

"Five Bears" and "Two Little Bear Cubs," p. 4 in **Kidstuff**, vol. 2, no. 8, "Bear-tivities!" edited by Sheila Debs. Lake Park, Fla.: GuideLines Press, 1983.

"The Small Koala Bear," p. 14 in **My Big Book of Fingerplays: A Fun-to-Say, Fun-to-Play Collection** by Daphne Hogstrom. il. by Sally Augustiny. Racine, Wis.: Western Publishing, 1974.

Filmstrip

Ask Mr. Bear by Marjorie Flack. il. by author. New York: Macmillan Library Services, 1974. 6 min.

The Bear's Bicycle by Emilie Warren McLeod. il. by David McPhail. Somers, N.Y.: Live Oak Media, 1977. 4 min. 15 sec.

Activities

"Old Mr. Bear," p. 5 in **Kidstuff**, vol. 2, no. 8, "Bear-tivities!" edited by Sheila Debs. Lake Park, Fla.: GuideLines Press, 1983. (This is a creative dramatics activity.)

Yummers

Stories about Food

PUBLICITY

A cornucopia or a picnic basket with colorful foods can grace your bulletin board, or you can cover the entire board with a collage of foods. Magazines are chock-full of pictures of food items.

Your posters can be cut in the shape of a gingerbread boy, a teapot, an apple, an ice cream cone, or a muffin. The same visuals can be used on your handouts.

PROGRAM PLAN

Introduction

Introduce the program: "Do you like to eat? I do! My favorite food is _____. What's your favorite food?" (Invite the children to share their favorites.)

There are many stories about food, all kinds of food: gingerbread boys, pie, jam sandwiches, cakes. . . . I'd like to share some of these stories with you now."

Read Aloud

The Turnip by Janina Domanska. il. by author. New York: Macmillan, 1969.

Introduce the story: "Grandmother and grandfather have planted a turnip. Now it's time to pull it out of the ground. But this is a stubborn and very unusual turnip. It doesn't seem to want to be pulled up." (This also adapts into a felt board story.)

Read Aloud

Gingerbread Boy by Paul Galdone. il. by author. New York: The Seabury Press, 1975.

Introduce the story: "You might not want to eat that enormous turnip, but I'm sure you would like to eat the star of our next story. And that's the problem: Everyone says gingerbread boys are for eating." (This also adapts into a felt board story.)

Fingerplay

"Make the Plum Pudding," p. 33 in **Listen! And Help Tell the Story** by Bernice Wells Carlson. il. by Burmah Burris. Nashville, Tenn.: Abingdon, 1965.

Introduce the story: "Let's pretend to make some food ourselves, some plum pudding."

Show the children how to do the fingerplay. Go through the individual actions. Then do the fingerplay together. Repeat. (Text of fingerplay is found in "Rainbow of Colors.")

Read Aloud

Gregory, the Terrible Eater by Mitchell Sharmat. il. by Jose Aruego and
Ariane Dewey. New York: Four Winds Press, 1980.

Introduce the story: "Gregory is a terrible eater! He likes orange juice, vegetables, and fruits. Why is that so terrible? Well, Gregory is a goat. He's supposed to like shoes, tin cans, and things of that sort. Will Gregory's parents be able to change his eating habits?"

Action Rhyme-Song

"Teapot," pp. 26-27 in **Ring a Ring O' Roses: Stories, Games and Finger Plays for Pre-School Children**, rev. ed. Flint, Mich.: Flint Public Library, 1981.

Introduce the rhyme-song: "A few minutes ago we made something to eat. Now let's make something to drink. Let's become a pot full of hot steaming tea."

It's time for a change of pace. Have the children stand, and make sure everyone has enough room to tip over. Many children will know this action rhyme, so have them join you right away. As with other action rhymes, you'll want to limit the number of children to about twenty or twenty-five unless you have a large space. The song is in:

Eye Winker, Tom Tinker, Chin Chopper by Tom Glazer. il. by Ron Himler.
Garden City, N.Y.: Doubleday, 1973, p. 36.

Sally Go Round the Sun: Three Hundred Children's Rhymes, Songs and Games by Edith Fowke. Garden City, N.Y.: Doubleday, 1969, p. 106.

Story Programs: A Source Book of Materials by Carolyn Sue Peterson and
Brenny Hall. Metuchen, N.J.: Scarecrow, 1980, p. 99.

Teapot

I'm a little teapot,
Short and stout.
Here's my handle,
And here's my spout.
(Place right hand on hip; extend left hand, palm out.)

When I get all steamed up,
I just shout:
"Tip me over, and pour me out."
(Bend to the left.)

I can change my handle
(Place left hand on hip, and extend right hand out.)

And my spout.
"Tip me over, and pour me out."
(Bend to the right.)

Book Talk

Nobody Stole the Pie by Sonia Levitin. il. by Fernando Krahn. New York: Harcourt Brace Jovanovich, 1980.

Introduce the story: "The town of Little Digby has a wonderful lollyberry tree, and every year a huge pie is made with the berries from the tree. All the townspeople are invited to eat a piece of the pie at the town festival, but this year is different. The hour of the festival arrives, and the people discover that the gigantic pie is gone. Everyone is in shock. The mayor wants to know who stole the pie. How could anyone take the pie without being seen? Get to the bottom of this mystery by having someone read this book to you at home."

The Giant Jam Sandwich with story and pictures by John V. Lord and verses by Janet Burroway. Boston: Houghton Mifflin, 1973.

Introduce the story: "Four million wasps flew into the town of Itching Down one day. What a problem! What can the townspeople do to get rid of the wasps? The people put their heads together and come up with a plan. For the plan to work, the people will need a giant loaf of bread; strawberry jam, lots of it; and a helicopter!"

The Duchess Bakes a Cake by Virginia Kahl. il. by author. New York: Scribner's, 1955.

Introduce the story: "The duchess is bored, so she decides to bake a cake. She puts everything into the mix: lots of yeast to make the batter rise, flour, sugar, almonds, raisins, eggs, and all sorts of berries and spices. She stirs it, pokes it, pinches it, and then sits on it! And the cake rises and rises higher and higher until the duchess is way above the castle. How will she ever get down?"

Don't Forget the Bacon by Pat Hutchins. il. by author. New York: Greenwillow Books, 1976.

Introduce the story: "What will the young boy in this book do? He forgot what his mother told him to get from the grocery store. Was he supposed to buy legs or pegs or eggs? A cape, a cake, a rake? How will he ever get it straight?"

The Shopping Basket by John Burningham. il. by author. New York: Thomas
   Y. Crowell, 1980.
Introduce the story: "A young boy's mother sends him to the store to buy several items. But he doesn't have the problem the boy in *Don't Forget the Bacon* has. No, this boy remembers what to buy. His problems start on the trip home. There are many animals waiting to get the food away from him. Can the boy outsmart the animals and bring the groceries safely to his mother?"

Activities

"Making Butter."
Introduce the activity: "We've talked about many foods today. We've even pretended to make food. Now, let's make some real food. Let's make butter. It's very easy to do."

For this activity, you need a glass jar, a pint of heavy cream, a strainer, a bowl, and crackers (with unsalted tops).

Before the program, place the cream in the glass jar, and shake it for about five minutes. Enlist some assistance so that you don't get a sore arm.

The children remain seated for this activity. If the group is small enough, they can stand around a low table. Let each child shake the jar several times. Be sure no one shakes so vigorously that he smacks himself with the jar! Within eight to ten minutes, a solid ball of butter will form. Open the jar, drain the excess liquid through the strainer and into a bowl, and put the butter on a plate. Let the children sample their efforts on a cracker. Yum!

Be sure to have copies of the "recipe" available for parents. Many of them will ask for instructions on how to make the butter at home.

Give the children a delicious memory of the program. Possible giveaways include small boxes of raisins, homemade gingerbread boys, and apples.

Note: Because there are so many excellent titles about food, you can narrow the focus of your program. Limit yourself to stories about pots, or do a program on fussy eaters. For the former topic, use *Strega Nona*, *Stone Soup*, *The Magic Cooking Pot*, and *Gustav the Gourmet Giant*. For the latter topic, use *Mrs. Pig's Bulk Buy*; *Lentil Soup*; *Gustav the Gourmet Giant*; *It's Your Turn, Roger!*; *Bread and Jam for Frances*; *Eat!*; and *Gregory, the Terrible Eater*. Full bibliographic information is given for these titles in Try This!

TRY THIS!

Read Aloud

Asbjørnsen, P. C., and Moe Jørgen. **The Runaway Pancake**. translated by Joan Tate. il. by Svend Otto S. New York: Larousse, 1980.

Asch, Frank. **Mooncake**. il. by author. Englewood Cliffs, N.J.: Prentice-Hall, 1983.

Brandenberg, Fritz. **Fresh Cider and Pie**. il. by author. New York: Macmillan, 1973.

Brown, Marcia. **The Bun: A Tale from Russia**. il. by author. New York: Harcourt Brace Jovanovich, 1972.

Brown, Marcia. **Stone Soup**. il. by author. New York: Scribner's, 1947. (This also adapts into a felt board story.)

Carle, Eric. **The Very Hungry Caterpillar**. il. by author. Cleveland, Ohio: William Collins and World Publishing, [1970]. (This also adapts into a felt board story.)

DePaola, Tomie. **The Magic Porridge Pot**. il. by author. Boston: Houghton Mifflin, 1976.

DePaola, Tomie. **Strega Nona: An Old Tale Retold**. il. by author. Englewood Cliffs, N.J.: Prentice-Hall, 1975.

Gaeddert, Lou Ann. **Gustav the Gourmet Giant**. il. by Steven Kellogg. New York: Dial Press, 1976.

Galdone, Paul. **The Little Red Hen**. il. by author. New York: The Seabury Press, 1973.

Gordon, Margaret. **The Supermarket Mice**. il. by author. New York: E. P. Dutton, 1984.

Gretz, Susanna. **It's Your Turn, Roger!** il. by author. New York: Dial Press, 1985.

Lasker, Joe. **Lentil Soup**. il. by author. Chicago: Albert Whitman, 1977.

Marshall, James. **Yummers!** il. by author. Boston: Houghton Mifflin, 1973.

Mosel, Arlene. **Funny Little Woman**. il. by Blair Lent. New York: E. P. Dutton, 1972.

Parker, Nancy Winslow. **Love from Aunt Betty**. il. by author. New York: Dodd, Mead, 1983.

Rayner, Mary. **Mrs. Pig's Bulk Buy**. il. by author. New York: Atheneum, 1981.

Rice, Eve. **Benny Bakes a Cake**. il. by author. New York: Greenwillow Books, 1981.

Scheer, Julian. **Rain Makes Applesauce**. il. by author. New York: Holiday House, 1964.

Sendak, Maurice. **In the Night Kitchen**. il. by author. New York: Harper & Row, 1970.

Tolstoy, Alexei. **The Great Big Enormous Turnip**. il. by Helen Oxenbury. New York: Franklin Watts, 1968.

Book Talk

Barrett, Judi. **Cloudy with a Chance of Meatballs**. il. by Ron Barrett. New York: Atheneum, 1978.

Delton, Judy. **Rabbit Finds a Way**. il. by Joe Lasker. New York: Crown, 1975.

DePaola, Tomie. **Pancakes for Breakfast.** il. by author. New York: Harcourt Brace Jovanovich, 1978. (This is a wordless book.)

DePaola, Tomie. **The Popcorn Book**. il. by author. New York: Holiday House, 1978. (This is a nonfiction title.)

Hoban, Russell. **Bread and Jam for Frances**. il. by Lillian Hoban. New York: Harper & Row, 1964.

McCloskey, Robert. **Blueberries for Sal**. il. by author. New York: Viking Press, 1948.

Nordqvist, Sven. **Pancake Pie**. il. by author. New York: William Morrow, 1984.

Paterson, Diane. **Eat!** il. by author. New York: Dial Press, 1975.

Watson, Wendy. **Lollipop**. il. by author. New York: Thomas Y. Crowell, 1976.

Young, Miriam Burt. **The Sugar Mouse Cake**. il. by Margaret Bloy Graham. New York: Scribner's, 1964.

Poetry

"One, One Cinnamon Bun," p. 24 in **Catch Me & Kiss Me and Say It Again**. rhymes by Clyde Watson. il. by Wendy Watson. New York: Philomel Books, 1978.

"Spaghetti, Spaghetti," pp. 16-19, "Chocolate Milk," pp. 20-21, and "Fudge," pp. 26-31 in **Rainy Rainy Saturday** by Jack Prelutsky. il. by Marilyn Hafner. New York: Greenwillow Books, 1980.

Fingerplay and Action Rhyme

"The Apple Tree," p. 24 in **Finger Plays That Motivate** by Don Peek. Minneapolis, Minn.: T. S. Denison, 1975.

"A Delicious Cake," p. 23, and "Pancake," p. 26 in **Ring a Ring O' Roses: Stories, Games and Finger Plays for Pre-School Children**, rev. ed. Flint, Mich.: Flint Public Library, 1981.

"Five Red Apples," p. 120 in **Rhymes for Fingers and Flannelboards** by Louise Binder Scott and J. J. Thompson. il. by Jean Flowers. Minneapolis, Minn.: Webster Publishing/T. S. Denison, 1960.

"In the Apple Tree," p. 22, and "Pop! Pop! Pop!" p. 106 in **Finger Frolics: Over 250 Fingerplays for Young Children from 3 Years**, rev. ed. compiled by Liz Cromwell, Dixie Hibner, and John R. Faitel. il. by Joan Lockwood. Livonia, Mich.: Partner Press, 1983.

"Making Stew," p. 4 in **Kidstuff**, vol. 2, no. 3, "Goodness How Delicious!" edited by Sheila Debs. Lake Park, Fla.: GuideLines Press, 1983.

Song

"The Muffin," p. 34 in **Singing Bee! A Collection of Favorite Children's Songs** compiled by Jane Hart. il. by Anita Lobel. New York: Lothrop, Lee & Shepard Books, 1982.

"Oh My Goodness" in **Father Fox's Feast of Songs**. words and music by Clyde Watson. il. by Wendy Watson. New York: Philomel Books, 1983, unpaged.

Westcott, Nadine. **I Know an Old Lady Who Swallowed a Fly**. il. by author. Boston: Little, Brown, 1980.

Film

The Gingerbread Man. Chicago: Perspective Films and Video, 1979. 10 min.

The Mole and the Lollipop. New York: Contemporary Films, McGraw-Hill, 1971. 9 min.

Activities

"Frosted Animals."

Take a box of animal crackers and a can of frosting. Let each child frost an animal or two and enjoy.

Happy Birthday
to You!

PUBLICITY

Create a poster in the shape of a party hat or gift package. Design your handouts to look like party invitations. Turn your bulletin board into a giant birthday cake, with program information written directly on it. You might choose to decorate your board with items associated with birthdays: cakes and candles, gifts, party hats, balloons, ice cream cones, and birthday cards. Or transform your bulletin board into a party invitation. Everyone can lift the flap on the invitation to reveal what's underneath—program information.

PROGRAM PLAN

You might want to create a party atmosphere with balloons, streamers, and a happy birthday banner. Wear a party hat, and provide hats for the children too. A word of caution: All this "fuss" might make some children too excitable. Know your group!

Introduction

Introduce the program: "All of us have birthdays, and today we're going to celebrate everyone's birthday.

Birthdays make me think of cake, presents, friends, parties and. . . . What do birthdays make you think of? (Give the children a chance to respond.) We're going to hear about many of the things you've mentioned in the stories I share with you today."

Read Aloud

The Secret Birthday Message by Eric Carle. il. by author. New York: Thomas Y. Crowell, 1972.

Introduce the story: "How exciting! The young boy in this story has received a secret message. If he follows the directions in the letter, he'll get a wonderful surprise. What could it be?"

This is a good book to draw children into the program because of its special and intriguing format—the pages have cutouts and are varied in shape.

Read Aloud

The Mysterious Tadpole by Steven Kellogg. il. by author. New York: Dial Press, 1977.

Introduce the story: "Every year Louis receives a special present from his Uncle McAllister who lives in Scotland. This year Louis receives what seems to be a very ordinary gift—until it starts to grow."

Read Aloud

Happy Birthday, Sam by Pat Hutchins. il. by author. New York: Greenwillow Books, 1978.

Introduce the story: "Sam is sure that having another birthday means he will be able to do all sorts of things he couldn't do before his birthday. Is this true?"

Fingerplay

"Five Birthday Candles," p. 25 in **Listen! And Help Tell the Story** by Bernice Wells Carlson. il. by Burmah Burris. Nashville, Tenn.: Abingdon, 1965.

Introduce the fingerplay: "One of the most enjoyable things to do at a birthday party is to blow out the candles on the birthday cake. Let's do that right now."

This fingerplay can be done with a very large group. The children won't learn all the words in one sitting, but they will enjoy blowing out the "candles." Show the children how to do the fingerplay as you recite it. Then have the children join you. Repeat.

Five Birthday Candles*

(Raise one hand with fingers extended. Starting with thumb,
lower one finger each time you blow out a candle.)

Five birthday candles;
Wish there were more.
Blow out one   (Blow quickly.)
Then there are four.

Four birthday candles
Pretty as can be.
Blow out one   (Blow quickly.)
Then there are three.

---

*From *Listen! And Help Tell the Story* by Bernice Wells Carlson. Copyright © 1965 by Abingdon Press. Used by permission.

Three birthday candles;
Mother bought them new.
Blow out one   (Blow quickly.)
Then there are two.

Two birthday candles —
Birthday cakes are fun.
Blow out one   (Blow quickly.)
Then there is one.

One birthday candle —
A birthday wish is fun.   (Pause.)
Blow out one   (Blow slowly.)
Then there is none.

Read Aloud

No Roses for Harry by Gene Zion. il. by Margaret Bloy Graham. New York: Harper & Row, 1958.

Introduce the story: "Animals celebrate their birthdays too. Today is Harry's birthday. But Harry isn't very happy with one of his presents. He'll do anything to get rid of this gift."

Read Aloud

Benjamin's 365 Birthdays by Judith Barrett. il. by Ron Barrett. New York: Atheneum, 1974.

Introduce the story: "Benjamin, unlike Harry, loves all his presents. He especially likes to open his presents. For Benjamin that's the best part. Why, he'd like to open presents all the time. Can he do that?"

Book Talk

Lyle and the Birthday Party by Bernard Waber. il. by author. Boston: Houghton Mifflin, 1966.

Introduce the story: "The Primm family is having a birthday party for their son Joshua. Lyle, their pet crocodile, is jealous. He wonders why the party can't be for him. And that's when Lyle's troubles begin. His problems include a broken drum and a stay in a hospital for humans."

A Birthday for Frances by Russell Hoban. il. by Lillian Hoban. New York: Harper & Row, 1968.

Introduce the story: "Frances is jealous too. Tomorrow is her sister Gloria's birthday. Frances wants the party for herself. She doesn't even want to give her sister a present. Will Frances ruin her sister's party, or will she be good and give her sister a present?"

Mr. Rabbit and the Lovely Present by Charlotte Zolotow. il. by Maurice Sendak. New York: Harper & Row, 1962.

Introduce the story: "The little girl in this story doesn't know what to get her mother for a birthday present, so she asks Mr. Rabbit for advice. And what a gift he helps her select! This present has something red, something orange, something yellow, something green, and something blue."

Mop Top by Don Freeman. il. by author. New York: Viking Press, 1955.

Introduce the story: "It's Mop Top's birthday, and his mom wants him to get a haircut. But Mop Top likes his wild lionlike hair. So instead of going to the barbershop, he hides in the grocery store. Mop Top makes one big mistake, though. He shouldn't have hidden behind the brooms."

Birthday Game

"Simon Says."

Enjoy a typical birthday game with the children. Ask the children to stand, and check to be sure that each child has ample room to move about. Explain that when you say "Simon says" to do something, they should do it. If you don't say "Simon says," then they shouldn't do what you say.

Below is a possible sequence; add your own commands, and continue the activity as long as the children are interested:

> Simon says raise your right hand.
> Simon says cluck like a chicken.
> Hop on one foot.
> Simon says jump up and down.
> Take a giant step forward.
> Clap your hands.
> Simon says clap your hands.
> Simon says touch your toes.
> Twirl around.
> Put your hand on your head.
> Sit down.
> Simon says sit down.
> Simon says shut your eyes.
> Simon says flap your arms like a bird.
> Touch your nose.
> Shout like a lion.
> Simon says shout like a lion.
> Simon says see you next week.

End the program on a festive note by handing out cupcakes to the children—their individual birthday cakes. Put the cupcakes in small paper bags so that the children can transport them home easily.

TRY THIS!

Read Aloud

Asch, Frank. **Happy Birthday, Moon!** il. by author. Englewood Cliffs, N.J.: Prentice-Hall, 1982.

Brandenberg, Franz. **A Secret for Grandmother's Birthday**. il. by Aliki. New York: Greenwillow Books, 1975.

Brandenberg, Franz. **Aunt Nina and Her Nephews and Nieces**. il. by Aliki. New York: Greenwillow Books, 1983.

Carrick, Carol. **Paul's Christmas Birthday**. il. by Donald Carrick. New York: Greenwillow Books, 1978.

Hughes, Shirley. **Alfie Gives a Hand**. il. by author. New York: Lothrop, Lee & Shepard Books, 1983.

Hutchins, Pat. **The Surprise Party**. il. by author. New York: Macmillan, 1969.

Keats, Ezra Jack. **A Letter to Amy**. il. by author. New York: Harper & Row, 1968.

Parker, Nancy Winslow. **Love from Uncle Clyde**. il. by author. New York: Dodd, Mead, 1977.

Rice, Eve. **Benny Bakes a Cake**. il. by author. New York: Greenwillow Books, 1981.

Book Talk

Brunhoff, Laurent de. **Babar's Birthday Surprise**. il. by author. New York: Random House, 1970.

Da Rif, Andrea. **The Blueberry Cake That Little Fox Baked**. il. by author. New York: Atheneum, 1984.

Emberley, Ed. **A Birthday Wish**. il. by author. Boston: Little, Brown, 1977. (This is a wordless book.)

Flack, Marjorie. **Ask Mr. Bear**. il. by author. New York: Macmillan, 1932.

Geisel, Theodore. **Happy Birthday to You!** il. by author. New York: Random House, 1959.

Kellogg, Steven. **Won't Somebody Play with Me?** il. by author. New York: Dial Press, 1972.

Nordqvist, Sven. **Pancake Pie**. il. by author. New York: William Morrow, 1984.

Wahl, Jan. **Margaret's Birthday**. il. by Mercer Mayer. New York: Four Winds Press, 1971.

Fingerplay and Action Rhyme

"Birthday Cake," p. 5 in **Kidstuff**, vol. 3, no. 12, "Happy Birthday!" edited by Sheila Debs. Lake Park, Fla.: GuideLines Press, 1985.

"Ten Little Candles," p. 60, and "What Am I Baking?" p. 62 in **Ring a Ring O' Roses: Stories, Games and Finger Plays for Pre-School Children**, rev. ed. Flint, Mich.: Flint Public Library, 1981.

Filmstrip

Happy Birthday, Moon! by Frank Asch. il. by author. Weston, Conn.: Weston Woods, 1983. 6 min.

A Letter to Amy by Ezra Jack Keats. il. by author. Weston, Conn.: Weston Woods, 1970. 6 min.

Activities

"Memory Game with Birthday Party Items."
Make items associated with birthdays out of felt. Place a few of the items on a felt board, and cover them with a cloth or a piece of poster board. Ask the children to recall what they saw. Do this several times with different combinations and numbers of items. Remember, you want the children to have a sense of accomplishment, so don't make it too difficult.
Here are some suggestions for items you can make out of felt: birthday cake, hat, clown, balloon, invitation, ice cream cone, present, candle, card, child dressed in party outfit, streamers, horn, a happy birthday banner.

—Developed by Paula Gaj Sitarz

"Pass the Present," p. 6 in **Kidstuff**, vol. 3, no. 12, "Happy Birthday!" edited by Sheila Debs. Lake Park, Fla.: GuideLines Press, 1985.

"Pin the Tail on the Donkey, or Put the Candle on the Birthday Cake."
    Make the donkey and the tail or the cake and the candle out of felt, so you don't have to worry about tape falling off the tail or the candle. During the program, put the donkey or the cake on a felt board. Blindfold each child in turn, and let each child try to pin the tail on the donkey or put the candle on the birthday cake.

Season's
Greetings
Christmas Stories

PUBLICITY

Turn your bulletin board into a giant gift package! Cover the board with gold or silver wrapping paper. Tack a piece of ribbon horizontally and one vertically over the paper; mark the intersection with a bow. Print program information on a large gift tag cut out in the shape of a sprig of holly.

Use a bell, a tree, an ornament, a candle, or a snowman as the visual for handouts and posters. You can also design a poster that looks like a giant gift tag.

You might wish to open this program to other groups of children from nursery and preschools.

PROGRAM PLAN

Paper chains in red and green provide a colorful decoration for the program area. Perhaps you have a small tree in the children's room? Bring in a wreath or a stuffed snowman.

Introduction

Encourage the children to respond to this question: "What do Christmas and the holidays make you think of?"

Continue in this way: "There are many stories about Christmas and the holidays. There are Christmas stories about friends, magic, food, Christmas trees, Santa Claus, parties, and presents. Let's enjoy some of them now."

Read Aloud

Tilly's Rescue by Faith Jaques. il. by author. New York: Atheneum, 1979.

Introduce the story: "This time of year, Christmastime, is a time to share, to be with people you love. That's what Tilly the wooden doll wants to do at Christmas. She wants to be with her friend Edward, the teddy bear. He's supposed to be at her house now, but he hasn't come. Where is he?"

Fingerplay

"Make the Plum Pudding," p. 33 in **Listen! And Help Tell the Story** by Bernice Wells Carlson. il. by Burmah Burris. Nashville, Tenn.: Abingdon, 1965.

Introduce the fingerplay: "Many people make plum pudding for Christmas. Let's make some ourselves."

If you've already used this fingerplay in the program on colors and food, have the children join you right away. Repeat the fingerplay. (Text of fingerplay is found in "Rainbow of Colors.")

Read Aloud

The Elves and the Shoemaker by Freya Littledale. il. by Brinton Turkle. New York: Four Winds Press, 1975.
Introduce the story: "The Christmas season is a time when magical things seem possible. Is magic at work in our next story?"

Fingerplay-Song

"Christmas Tree," p. 93 in **Let's Do Fingerplays** by Marion F. Grayson. il. by Nancy Weyl. Washington, D.C.: Robert B. Luce, 1962.
Introduce the fingerplay-song: "Christmas also makes me think of trees— with ornaments, toys, and lights on them."
You can turn this fingerplay into a song by singing it to the tune of "Mulberry Bush." Sing the tune to the children, and show them how to do the various motions. Then invite the children to do the actions with you and to sing as much of the song as they can. Try it again. Make up additional verses.

Read Aloud

A Visit from St. Nicholas: 'Twas the Night before Christmas by Clement C. Moore. il. by Paul Galdone. New York: McGraw-Hill, 1968.
Introduce the story: "This is the story of one family's special Christmas Eve Visitor."

Book Talk

Bah! Humbug? by Lorna Balian. il. by author. Nashville, Tenn.: Abingdon, 1977.
Introduce the story: "Margie is sure that Santa Claus is real. Her brother Arthur says there is no Santa. But Arthur's been wrong lots of times, so maybe he'll be wrong again. Find out who is right when Arthur sets a trap for Santa."

Mr. Willoby's Christmas Tree by Robert Barry. il. by Paul Galdone. New York: McGraw-Hill, 1963.
Introduce the story: "Mr. Willoby's tree is full and fresh but much too tall. Something must go! So Mr. Willoby cuts off the top of his tree. Wouldn't he be surprised to learn that this tree top becomes the tree for a maid, a gardener, a bear family, a fox family, a rabbit family, and a mouse family? Find out how that happens by sharing this story with someone at home."

Christmas Tree*

Here stands a lovely Christmas tree,
Christmas tree, Christmas tree,
(Hold hands up, fingertips touching.)

Here stands a lovely Christmas tree,
So early in the morning.

Here is a horn for the Christmas tree,
Christmas tree, Christmas tree,
(Hold fist to mouth and blow.)

Here is a horn for the Christmas tree,
So early in the morning.

Here is a drum for the Christmas tree,
Christmas tree, Christmas tree,
(Beat drum.)

Here is a drum for the Christmas tree,
So early in the morning.

Here are the lights for the Christmas tree,
Christmas tree, Christmas tree,
(Flutter fingers.)

Here are the lights for the Christmas tree,
So early in the morning.

Here stands a lovely Christmas tree,
Christmas tree, Christmas tree,
(Hold hands up, fingertips touching.)

Here stands a lovely Christmas tree
So early in the morning.

*From *Let's Do Fingerplays* by Marion F. Grayson. Copyright © 1962 by Robert B. Luce. Used by permission.

Arthur's Christmas Cookies by Lillian Hoban. il. by author. New York: Harper & Row, 1972.

Introduce the story: "It's Christmastime! Arthur has no money to buy Christmas presents, so he decides to bake cookies to give to his friends. But something goes wrong, very wrong. Arthur's cookies are as hard as rocks when they come out of the oven. How did that happen? Everyone is waiting to enjoy the cookies, but they can't be eaten. Now what will Arthur give his friends as presents?"

The Christmas Party by Adrienne Adams. il. by author. New York: Scribner's, 1978.

Introduce the story: "A group of young rabbits want Orson to help them plan a Christmas party. Orson doesn't want to help. He thinks he'll end up doing all the work for the party. But will he? Who knows! If Orson does help out, maybe he'll have a very special Christmas."

The Christmas Piñata by Jack Kent. il. by author. New York: Parents Magazine Press, 1975.

Introduce the story: "This is the story of a poor little pot that has a crack in it. Instead of being decorated and taken to market to be sold, the pot is left in a corner. The pot is sure that no one wants it, but Maria notices the pot, and she knows what it would be just right for."

Filmstrip

Morris's Disappearing Bag by Rosemary Wells. il. by author. Weston, Conn.: Weston Woods, 1978. 6 min.

Introduce the film: "Morris's brothers and sisters won't let him play with their Christmas presents. But wait until they see Morris's special Christmas present. They'll probably offer Morris anything to use it."

Christmas Song

Sing traditional songs such as "Santa Claus Is Coming to Town," "Rudolph the Red Nosed Reindeer," "We Wish You a Merry Christmas," and "Jingle Bells." If someone on the staff plays an instrument (or perhaps you do), ask her to accompany you on these tunes.

You might want to invite the parents and care givers to join the children for this segment of the program.

"Jingle Bells," pp. 150-51, and "We Wish You a Merry Christmas," p. 153 in **Singing Bee! A Collection of Favorite Children's Songs** compiled by Jane Hart. il. by Anita Lobel. New York: Lothrop, Lee & Shepard Books, 1982.

Activities

"The Piñata."

Explain to the children that each country has its own Christmas customs. In Mexico the children break a piñata that is hanging from the ceiling or from a pole. The children break the piñata with a long stick. It's not as easy as it sounds because the children are blindfolded when they try to break the piñata.

Show the children a piñata, and describe how it was made. Tell the children that they won't break this piñata but that they will receive the same goodies the children in Mexico get after they break the piñata.

Give each child a small bag of goodies and trinkets, such as balloons (deflated), Christmas cards, homemade cookies, small boxes of raisins, and bookmarks.

You can have the children break the piñata in the traditional way, but the time I tried it, the activity got out of hand when the children started grabbing for the goodies on the floor.

You'll find clear and easy instructions on making a piñata in *Piñatas* by Virginia Brock. il. by Anne Marie Jauss. Nashville, Tenn.: Abingdon, 1966. This book includes instructions for making piñatas in the shape of a donkey, a birthday cake, a star, and a Santa Claus.

TRY THIS!

Read Aloud

Brown, Marc. **Arthur's Christmas**. il. by author. Boston: Little, Brown, 1984.

Carrick, Carol. **Paul's Christmas Birthday**. il. by Donald Carrick. New York: Greenwillow Books, 1978.

Galdone, Paul, reteller. **The Elves and the Shoemaker**. il. by Paul Galdone. New York: Ticknor & Fields/Houghton Mifflin, 1984.

Gay, Michel. **The Christmas Wolf**. il. by author. New York: Greenwillow Books, 1980.

Holabird, Katharine. **Angelina's Christmas**. il. by Helen Craig. New York: Crown, 1985.

Hutchins, Pat. **The Silver Christmas Tree**. il. by author. New York: Macmillan, 1974.

Kroll, Steven. **Santa's Crash Bang Christmas**. il. by Tomie dePaola. New York: Holiday House, 1977.

Merriam, Eve. **The Christmas Box**. il. by David Small. New York: William Morrow, 1985.

Moore, Clement C. **The Night before Christmas**. il. by Anita Lobel. New York: Alfred A. Knopf, 1984.

Moore, Clement C. **The Night before Christmas**. il. by Tomie dePaola. New York: Holiday House, 1980.

Olson, Arielle North. **Hurry Home, Grandma!** il. by Lydia Dabcovitch. New York: E. P. Dutton, 1984.

Stevenson, James. **The Night after Christmas**. il. by author. New York: Greenwillow Books, 1981.

Book Talk

Bemelmans, Ludwig. **Madeline's Christmas**. il. by author. New York: Viking Kestrel, 1985.

Gammell, Stephen. **Wake Up, Bear . . . It's Christmas!** il. by author. New York: Lothrop, Lee & Shepard Books, 1981.

Gantschev, Ivan. **The Christmas Train**. translated from German by Karen M. Klockner. il. by author. Boston: Little, Brown, 1984.

Gibbons, Gail. **Christmas Time**. il. by author. New York: Holiday House, 1982. (This is a nonfiction title.)

Noble, Trinka Hakes. **Apple Tree Christmas**. il. by author. New York: Dial Press, 1984.

Radin, Ruth Yaffe. **A Winter Place**. paintings by Mattie Lou O'Kelley. Boston: Little, Brown, 1982.

Schweninger, Ann. **Christmas Secrets**. il. by author. New York: Viking Kestrel, 1984.

Spier, Peter. **Peter Spier's Christmas!** il. by author. Garden City, N.Y.: Doubleday, 1983.

Wells, Rosemary. **Morris's Disappearing Bag: A Christmas Story**. il. by author. New York: Dial Press, 1975.

Wildsmith, Brian. **Brian Wildsmith's The Twelve Days of Christmas**. il. by author. New York: Franklin Watts, 1972.

Other Story Forms

"Santa Claus," pp. 8-9 in **Lots More Tell and Draw Stories** by Margaret S. Olson. Minneapolis, Minn.: Arts & Crafts Unlimited, 1973.

Poetry

Prelutsky, Jack. **It's Christmas**. il. by Marilyn Hafner. New York: Greenwillow Books, 1981.

Fingerplay and Action Rhyme

"Here's the Chimney," p. 94 in **Let's Do Fingerplays** by Marion F. Grayson. il. by Nancy Weyl. Washington, D.C.: Robert B. Luce, 1962.

Song

"Little Jack Horner," p. 36 in **Singing Bee! A Collection of Favorite Children's Songs** compiled by Jane Hart. il. by Anita Lobel. New York: Lothrop, Lee & Shepard Books, 1982.

Film

The Mole and the Christmas Tree. New York: Phoenix Films & Video, 1977. 6 min.

Hark! Hark!
The Dogs Do Bark

PUBLICITY

Hand out bookmarks cut in the shape of a dog bone to parents and their young children. Be sure to include program information on them. A dog dish with program information on it surrounded by dog bones is an easy bulletin board to create. Or fashion a large dog's head with big floppy ears out of felt. Simpler still, cut out pictures of dogs from magazines, and tack them on your bulletin board.

Invite children to bring their favorite stuffed toy dogs to the program.

PROGRAM PLAN

Introduction

Talk about the different sizes and shapes of dogs and the personalities they have. Encourage the children to discuss their dogs, both toy and real.

Poetry

"Oh Where, Oh Where?" "Old Mother Hubbard," "Hey Diddle Diddle," "There Was a Little Dog," "Dandy," "Little Bingo," and "Bow, Wow, Wow" in **Hark! Hark! The Dogs Do Bark and Other Rhymes about Dogs** edited by Lenore Blegvad. il. by Erik Blegvad. New York: Atheneum, 1976, unpaged.

Introduce the poems: "Many poems have been written about dogs, and here are some that you might have heard before."

These poems are quite short, so say one, then repeat it. Invite the children to join you on the repeat.

Read Aloud

David and Dog by Shirley Hughes. il. by author. Englewood Cliffs, N.J.: Prentice-Hall, 1978.

Introduce the story: "David loves Dog, his stuffed animal. He takes Dog everywhere he goes. So what would David do if anything ever happened to Dog?"

Read Aloud

Benjy's Dog House by Margaret Bloy Graham. il. by author. New York: Harper & Row, 1973.

Introduce the story: "The children's parents decide that Benjy the dog should sleep outdoors instead of inside with the children. Benjy doesn't like that idea at all, and he decides to do something about it."

Fingerplay

"Ten Fingers," p. 10 in **Ring a Ring O' Roses: Stories, Games and Finger Plays for Pre-School Children**, rev. ed. Flint, Mich.: Flint Public Library, 1981.

By now the children are quite familiar with this hand rhyme. Ask them to join you right away. Repeat. More and more of the children will start to recite the words. (Text of fingerplay is found in "Carnival of the Animals: An Introductory Program.")

Fingerplay

"Clap Your Hands," p. 10 in **Let's Do Fingerplays** by Marion F. Grayson. il. by Nancy Weyl. Washington, D.C.: Robert B. Luce, 1962.

In this fingerplay, the children repeat what you do and say, so there is no need to demonstrate this first. This fingerplay is quite brief, so be sure to repeat it.

Clap Your Hands*

(Perform actions as indicated by rhyme.)

Clap your hands, clap your hands,
Clap them just like me.

Touch your shoulders, touch your shoulders,
Touch them just like me.

Tap your knees, tap your knees,
Tap them just like me.

Shake your head, shake your head,
Shake it just like me.

Clap your hands, clap your hands,
Now let them quiet be.

---

*From *Let's Do Fingerplays* by Marion F. Grayson. Copyright © 1962 by Robert B. Luce. Used by permission.

Fingerplay

"Five Little Puppies," p. 36 in **Rhymes for Fingers and Flannelboards** by
Louise Binder Scott and J. J. Thompson. Minneapolis, Minn.: Webster
Publishing/T. S. Denison, 1960.
This is a counting hand rhyme—the children count down the puppies on
their fingers from five to one. It's easy to do. Show how it's done once, and
then have the children join in. If they are interested, repeat.

Five Little Puppies*

Five little puppies were playing in the sun;
(Hold up hands, fingers extended.)

This one saw a rabbit, and he began to run;
(Bend down first finger.)

This one saw a butterfly, and he began to race;
(Bend down second finger.)

This one saw a pussy cat, and he began to chase;
(Bend down third finger.)

This one tried to catch his tail, and he went round and
     round;
(Bend down fourth finger.)

This one was so quiet, he never made a sound.
(Bend down thumb.)

Read Aloud

Harry the Dirty Dog by Gene Zion. il. by Margaret Bloy Graham. New York:
Harper & Row, 1956.
Introduce the story: "If there's one thing Harry doesn't like, it's taking a
bath. He'll do anything not to have to get into that soapy water. But after what
happens to Harry, he might decide that taking a bath isn't so bad."

---

*From *Rhymes for Fingers and Flannelboards* by Louise Binder Scott and J. J. Thompson. Copyright © 1960 by T. S. Denison and Company. Used by permission.

Read Aloud

Whistle for Willie by Ezra Jack Keats. il. by author. New York: Viking Press, 1964.

Introduce the story: "Peter wants to whistle in the worst way. Why, then he could whistle for his dog Willie. Wouldn't that be fun! But whistling isn't as easy as it looks."

Book Talk

Poofy Loves Company by Nancy Winslow Parker. il. by author. New York: Dodd, Mead, 1980.

Introduce the story: "Watch out when you visit the nice lady who lives down the street. Her dog Poofy is cuddly and lovable, but he also has a mind of his own. He knows what he wants, and he goes after it. Sally will have to watch her things carefully, or Poofy will take everything she has—and knock her down too."

Pinkerton, Behave! by Steven Kellogg. il. by author. New York: Dial Press, 1979.

Introduce the story: "Pinkerton is lovable, too, but he's always doing the wrong thing, so the family sends him to obedience school. Pinkerton doesn't get things right there either. Fetch! Come! Attack! He gets them all mixed up. But somehow, when it counts, Pinkerton does the wrong thing, and it comes out right."

Nothing-at-All by Wanda Gag. il. by author. New York: Coward, McCann & Geoghegan, 1941.

Introduce the story: "Once upon a time three dogs lived together. One of them was invisible, and he was called Nothing-at-All. One day a boy and a girl took home the two puppies they could see. Nothing-at-All was left behind. He tried to catch up with the others, but he couldn't. Nothing-at-All decided then and there that he'd like people to be able to see him. Maybe then the boy and girl would take him home too. But how could Nothing-at-All become visible?"

Old Mother Hubbard and Her Dog. il. by Evaline Ness. New York: Holt, Rinehart and Winston, 1972.

Introduce the story: "Every time Mother Hubbard goes out or does something, she comes back to find her dog doing the strangest things. Have you ever seen a dog standing on his head? Riding a goat? Smoking a pipe? Dancing? You'll see this dog do all that and more if you share this book with someone at home."

TRY THIS!

Read Aloud

Batherman, Muriel. **Some Things You Should Know about My Dog**. il. by author. Englewood Cliffs, N.J.: Prentice-Hall, 1976.

DePaola, Tomie. **The Comic Adventures of Old Mother Hubbard and Her Dog**. il. by author. New York: Harcourt Brace Jovanovich, 1981.

Dunrea, Olivier. **Fergus and Bridey**. il. by author. New York: Holiday House, 1985.

Flack, Marjorie. **Angus and the Ducks**. il. by author. Garden City, N.Y.: Doubleday, 1930.

Gackenbach, Dick. **A Bag Full of Pups**. il. by author. New York: Ticknor & Fields/Houghton Mifflin, 1981.

Gackenbach, Dick. **Claude & Pepper**. il. by author. New York: The Seabury Press, 1976.

Gackenbach, Dick. **Pepper and All the Legs**. il. by author. Boston: Houghton Mifflin, 1978.

Graham, Margaret Bloy. **Benjy & the Barking Bird**. il. by author. New York: Harper & Row, 1971.

Graham, Margaret Bloy. **Benjy's Boat Trip**. il. by author. New York: Harper & Row, 1977.

Martin, Charles E. **Dunkel Takes a Walk**. il. by author. New York: Greenwillow Books, 1983.

Modell, Frank. **Tooley! Tooley!** il. by author. New York: Greenwillow Books, 1979.

Stadler, John. **Hector the Accordian-Nosed Dog**. Scarsdale, N.Y.: Bradbury Press, 1983.

Zion, Gene. **Harry by the Sea**. il. by Margaret Bloy Graham. New York: Harper & Row, 1965.

Zion, Gene. **No Roses for Harry**. il. by Margaret Bloy Graham. New York: Harper & Row, 1958.

Book Talk

Alexander, Martha. **Bobo's Dream**. il. by author. New York: Dial Press, 1970. (This is a wordless book.)

Freeman, Don. **Ski Pup**. il. by author. New York: Viking Press, 1963.

Keats, Ezra Jack. **Pssst! Doggie** — . il. by author. New York: Franklin Watts, 1973. (This is an almost wordless book.)

Kellogg, Steven. **Tallyho, Pinkerton!** il. by author. New York: Dial Press, 1982.

Lipkind, William, and Nicolas Mordvinoff. **Finders Keepers**. il. by authors. New York: Harcourt Brace Jovanovich, 1951.

Numeroff, Laura Joffe. **Digger**. il. by author. New York: E. P. Dutton, 1983.

Tanaka, Hideyuki. **The Happy Dog**. il. by author. New York: Atheneum, 1983. (This is a wordless book.)

Wildsmith, Brian. **Give a Dog a Bone**. il. by author. New York: Pantheon Books, 1985.

Zion, Gene. **Harry & the Lady Next Door**. il. by Margaret Bloy Graham. New York: Harper & Row, 1960.

Other Story Forms

"Frankie and the Cat," pp. 43-45 in **Tell and Draw Stories** by Margaret J. Olson. Minneapolis, Minn.: Creative Storytime Press, 1963.

Poetry

"My Puppy," p. 20 by Aileen Fisher in **A Child's First Book of Poems**. il. by Cyndy Szekeres. Racine, Wis.: Western Publishing, 1981.

Fingerplay and Action Rhyme

"Poor Dog! Poor Mo!" p. 56 in **Listen! And Help Tell the Story** by Bernice Wells Carlson. il. by Burmah Burris. Nashville, Tenn.: Abingdon, 1965.

"Puppy Dogs," p. 20 in **Ring a Ring O' Roses: Stories, Games and Finger Plays for Pre-School Children**, rev. ed. Flint, Mich.: Flint Public Library, 1981.

Song

"BINGO," p. 13 in **Eye Winker, Tom Tinker, Chin Chopper** by Tom Glazer. il. by Ron Himler. Garden City, N.Y.: Doubleday, 1973.

"Where, Oh Where Has My Little Dog Gone?" p. 114 in **Singing Bee! A Collection of Favorite Children's Songs** compiled by Jane Hart. il. by Anita Lobel. New York: Lothrop, Lee & Shepard Books, 1982.

Film

Angus Lost. New York: Phoenix Films & Video, 1982. 11 min.

Things That
Go

PUBLICITY

Publicize this program with posters cut out in the shape of a train car, a truck, a hot air balloon, a bus, or a rocket. Use one of these visuals for your handouts too. A hot air balloon or a long train can herald program information on your bulletin board. Or cover your board with a collage that depicts various modes of transportation. Use pictures cut from old magazines.

PROGRAM PLAN

Introduction

Introduce the program with brief talks about the following books. Show the illustrations in each book that correspond to what you're talking about.

Freight Train by Donald Crews. il. by author. New York: Greenwillow Books, 1978.

Introduce the story: "In this book you can follow a colorful train on its journey through tunnels, over bridges, and by cities."

Truck by Donald Crews. il. by author. New York: Greenwillow Books, 1980.

Introduce the story: "Follow the adventures of a trailer truck from loading—through tunnels, over bridges, through rain, and up and down hills—to unloading. And find out what important cargo it's carrying."

Airport by Byron Barton. il. by author. New York: Thomas Y. Crowell, 1982.

Introduce the story: "Take a peek at all the activities that take place at an airport. They include loading baggage, getting tickets, boarding the plane, and visiting the cockpit."

Continue the introduction by asking the children to name other things that go or things that get you places. Be sure that you, or they, mention bicycles, boats, buses, and cars. These are the other vehicles that are mentioned in the program.

Read Aloud

Henry, the Castaway by Mark Taylor. il. by Graham Booth. New York: Atheneum, 1972.

Introduce the story: "Henry is an explorer. Today, he and his dog Laird Angus McAngus are exploring a river. What they find there is a canoe. It looks safe enough, but it gets them into a lot of trouble."

Read Aloud

The Hippo Boat by Eriko Kishida. il. by Chiyoko Nakatani. Cleveland, Ohio: William Collins and World Publishing, 1968.

Introduce the story: "The strangest things can be used for getting from one place to another, especially when there's danger." (This adapts well into a felt board story.)

Fingerplay-Song

"Wheels on the Bus," pp. 74-75 in **Ring a Ring O' Roses: Stories, Games and Finger Plays for Pre-School Children**, rev. ed. Flint, Mich.: Flint Public Library, 1981.

Introduce the fingerplay-song: "So much happens on the bus when you go for a ride! You just have to look and listen."

Sing or say the refrain of the rhyme to the children, and demonstrate the accompanying motions. Briefly show how the actions are done for each verse. Put all the pieces of the rhyme together, and invite the children to join you. Some of the children will know this rhyme, and all of them will find the actions easy enough to follow. Repeat the verses that the children particularly enjoy, and ask them to make up additional verses. The song is found in:

Eye Winker, Tom Tinker, Chin Chopper by Tom Glazer. il. by Ron Himler. Garden City, N.Y.: Doubleday, 1973, pp. 16-17.

Wheels on the Bus

(Suit actions to words.)

The wheels on the bus go round and round,
Round and round, round and round.
The wheels on the bus go round and round,
All through the town.

The people on the bus go up and down,
Up and down, up and down.
The people on the bus go up and down,
All through the town.

The money on the bus goes clink, clank, clunk,
Clink, clank, clunk.
The money on the bus goes clink, clank, clunk,
All through the town.

The driver on the bus says, "Move on back," etc.

The children on the bus say, "Yak, yak, yak," etc.

The mothers on the bus say, "Sh, sh, shh," etc.

The wipers on the bus go swish, swish, swish, etc.

The horn on the bus goes honk, honk, honk, etc.

The wheels on the bus go round and round,
Round and round, round and round.
The wheels on the bus go round and round,
All through the town.

Read Aloud

Mr. Gumpy's Motor Car by John Burningham. il. by author. New York:
Thomas Y. Crowell, 1973.
Introduce the story: "Buses are meant to hold many people. But what
happens when you try to put lots of people and animals in a car, . . . and it
rains?"

Read Aloud

One-Eyed Jake by Pat Hutchins. il. by author. New York: Greenwillow
Books, 1979.
Introduce the story: "Lots of things seem to happen on boats, don't they?
Take the pirate One-Eyed Jake. He thinks he can rob all the other boats of
their treasures whenever he feels like it. But can he?"

Book Talk

Everyday Train by Amy Ehrlich. il. by Martha Alexander. New York: Dial
Press, 1977.
Introduce the story: "Jane is a lucky girl. A train runs by the back of her
yard every day. She loves it! Jane runs to meet the train when she hears its
whistle. She waves at the engineer as the engine whooshes by, and she even
plays a very special game with the train."

Wild Baby Goes to Sea by Barbro Lindgren. translated by Jack Prelutsky. il.
by Eva Erikkson. New York: Greenwillow Books, 1983.
Introduce the story: "While mother cleans the house, wild baby turns a
wooden box into a boat and sails away. He saves a mouse who falls overboard,
he wards off a hungry fish, he sails into a whale's mouth, and he faces a storm.

Wild Baby has other adventures, too, before he returns home safely to his mother."

Mike Mulligan and His Steam Shovel by Virginia Lee Burton. Boston: Houghton Mifflin, 1939, 1967.

Introduce the story: "Poor Mike Mulligan and his steam shovel Mary Anne. They can't find a job anywhere. No one wants to hire a steam shovel now that there are modern shovels. But one day Mike Mulligan sees an ad in the newspaper — the people in Poppersville need to have a cellar dug for the new town hall. Can Mary Anne and Mike Mulligan do the job? In one day?"

Filmstrip

Curious George Rides a Bike by H. A. Rey. il. by author. Weston, Conn.: Weston Woods, n.d. 14 min.

Introduce the film: "When the man with the yellow hat gives Curious George a bicycle, George can't ride it carefully the way he's told to. Oh, no. He has to see what else he can do with it — and that's when his troubles begin."

Fingerplay

"Johnny's Ride," p. 23 in **Listen! And Help Tell the Story** by Bernice Wells Carlson. il. by Burmah Burris. Nashville, Tenn.: Abingdon, 1965.

This is a very easy rhyme to share. You can do this with a very large group too. Demonstrate the rhyme for the children, and then invite them to join you. They'll want to do it again and again.

Johnny's Ride*

Johnny looked at the moon.	(Stretch arms over head. Hold hands in the shape of a moon.)
Johnny looked at the stars.	(With arms still lifted, wiggle fingers for twinkling stars.)
Johnny got in a rocket.	(Lower arms to waist. Place palms and fingers together in shape of a rocket cone.)

---

*From *Listen! And Help Tell the Story* by Bernice Wells Carlson. Copyright © 1965 by Abingdon Press. Used by permission.

Johnny went up to Mars.   (With hands still together,
                                 lift arms quickly as high as
                                 you can over your head.)

Action Rhyme

"Space Rocket," p. 53 in **Listen! And Help Tell the Story** by Bernice Wells
    Carlson. il. by Burmah Burris. Nashville, Tenn.: Abingdon, 1965.
    Introduce the rhyme: "Let's really blast off this time!"
    Again, this is a very easy rhyme and a great way to end your program —
with everyone blasting off. Demonstrate once, and then invite the children to
blast off too. Repeat several times.

Space Rocket*

(Sit with elbows close to the body and hands held in front
    with tips of fingers touching to form cone of a rocket.)

Inside a rocket ship,
Just enough room.
Here comes the countdown —
10, 9, 8, 7, 6, 5, 4, 3, 2, 1, 0,
And Zoo-o-o-o-o-o-om!   (Stand up and raise arms
                                     as high as possible with
                                     fingers still held together
                                     like the cone of a rocket.)

TRY THIS!

Read Aloud

Burningham, John. **Mr. Gumpy's Outing**. il. by author. New York: Holt,
    Rinehart and Winston, 1971.

Calhoun, Mary. **Hot-Air Henry**. il. by Erick Ingraham. New York: William
    Morrow, 1981.

Douglass, Barbara. **The Great Town & Country Bicycle Balloon Chase**. il. by
    Carol Newsom. New York: Lothrop, Lee & Shepard Books, 1984.

Piper, Watty. **The Little Engine That Could**. il. by George Hauman and Doris Hauman. New York: Platt & Munk Publishers, 1930.

Book Talk

Alexander, Anne. **ABC of Cars and Trucks**. il. by Ninon. Garden City, N.Y.: Doubleday, 1956.

Burton, Virginia Lee. **Choo Choo: The Story of a Little Engine Who Ran Away**. il. by author. Boston: Houghton Mifflin, 1937.

Crews, Donald. **Harbor**. il. by author. New York: Greenwillow Books, 1982.

Fuchs, Erich. **Journey to the Moon**. il. by author. New York: Delacorte Press, 1969. (This is a nonfiction title.)

Gibbons, Gail. **Boat Book**. il. by author. New York: Holiday House, 1983.

Gibbons, Gail. **Flying**. il. by author. New York: Holiday House, 1986. (This is a nonfiction title.)

Gibbons, Gail. **Trucks**. il. by author. New York: Thomas Y. Crowell, 1981. (This is a nonfiction title.)

Gramatky, Hardie. **Little Toot**. il. by author. New York: Putnam, 1939, 1967.

Haas, Irene. **The Maggie B**. il. by author. New York: Atheneum, 1975.

Kessler, Ethel, and Leonard Kessler. **All Aboard the Train**. il. by authors. Garden City, N.Y.: Doubleday, 1964.

Maestro, Betty, and Ellen DelVecchio. **Big City Port**. il. by Guilio Maestro. New York: Four Winds Press, 1983.

McLeod, Emilie W. **The Bear's Bicycle**. il. by David McPhail. Boston: Little, Brown, 1975.

McPhail, David. **The Train**. il. by author. Boston: Little, Brown, 1977.

Provensen, Alice, and Martin Provensen. **The Glorious Flight: Across the Channel with Louis Bleriot**. New York: Viking Press, 1983.

Rey, H. A. **Curious George Rides a Bike**. il. by author. Boston: Houghton Mifflin, 1952.

Rockwell, Anne, and Harlow Rockwell. **Thruway**. il. by authors. New York: Macmillan, 1972.

Sattler, Helen Roney. **Train Whistles: A Language in Code**. il. by Tom Funk. New York: Lothrop, Lee & Shepard Books, 1977. (This is a nonfiction title.)

Fingerplay and Action Rhyme

"Choo Choo Train," p. 23, and "Row, Row, Row Your Boats," p. 26 in **Let's Do Fingerplays** by Marion F. Grayson. il. by Nancy Weyl. Washington, D.C.: Robert B. Luce, 1962.

"Ring around the Rocket Ship," p. 35, and "Steam Shovel," p. 74 in **Ring a Ring O' Roses: Stories, Games and Finger Plays for Pre-School Children**, rev. ed. Flint, Mich.: Flint Public Library, 1981.

Song

"Row, Row, Row Your Boat," p. 135 in **Singing Bee! A Collection of Children's Favorites** compiled by Jane Hart. il. by Anita Lobel. New York: Lothrop, Lee & Shepard Books, 1982.

Filmstrip

Mr. Gumpy's Outing by John Burningham. il. by author. Weston, Conn.: Weston Woods, 1973. 5 min.

Film

Little Toot. Burbank, Calif.: Walt Disney Company, 1948. 9 min.

The Little Train. Oak Park, Ill.: Film Images, 1971. 10 min.

The Mole and the Bulldozer. New York: Phoenix Films & Video, 1975. 7 min.

The Mole and the Car. New York: Phoenix Films & Video, 1976. 16 min.

The Mole and the Rocket. New York: Phoenix Films & Video, 1973. 10 min.

Activities

"Moon Ride," p. 73 in **Ring a Ring O' Roses: Stories, Games and Finger Plays for Pre-School Children**, rev. ed. Flint, Mich.: Flint Public Library, 1981.

Strange
Creatures

PUBLICITY

Let your imagination run wild! Draw silly and fanciful creatures—heads or full bodies—for your bulletin board. Fashion the creatures out of felt or construction paper. Or ask children to draw monsters for the board. Create a simple robot design for your handouts, or use a monster's head as the visual for handouts and posters.

PROGRAM PLAN

Introduction

Introduce the program: "Monsters and strange creatures come in all shapes and sizes. Some people think they're funny; some think they're silly. We know that they're make believe."

Read Aloud

Harry by the Sea by Gene Zion. il. by Margaret Bloy Graham. New York: Harper & Row, 1965.
Introduce the story: "How can a white dog with black spots turn into a monster? Let's join Harry on the beach and find out."

Read Aloud

Harry and the Terrible Whatzit by Dick Gackenbach. il. by author. Boston: Houghton Mifflin, 1977.
Introduce the story: "Let's meet another Harry—not a dog but a young boy. This Harry doesn't turn into a monster; he meets up with a monster!"

Read Aloud-Action Rhyme

Seven Little Monsters by Maurice Sendak. il. by author. New York: Harper & Row, 1977.
Share this very short book with the children, and then turn it into an action rhyme. Have the children count each of the seven monsters on their fingers, and pantomime the monsters' actions. This can be done while seated with any size group. Be sure to demonstrate the actions first.

Read Aloud

Where the Wild Things Are by Maurice Sendak. il. by author. New York: Harper & Row, 1963.

Introduce the story: "Max, like Harry, isn't afraid of monsters—not even monsters with yellow eyes."

Read Aloud

There's a Nightmare in My Closet by Mercer Mayer. il. by author. New York: Dial Press, 1968.

Introduce the story: "Meet another young person who isn't afraid of strange creatures. He must know—like we do—that they aren't real."

Action Rhyme

"The Robot," p. 11 in **My Big Book of Fingerplays: A Fun-to-Say, Fun-to-Play Collection** by Daphne Hogstrom. il. by Sally Augustiny. Racine, Wis.: Western Publishing, 1974.

If you have a lot of space, you can do this action rhyme with a large group. If space is limited, use this with about twenty to twenty-five children. Say the rhyme and demonstrate the actions. Next, have the children join you in doing the actions. Say the two lines that the robot recites slowly and repeatedly, so the children can chime in on them.

The Robot*

Here's a robot,
Big and strong.
Watch him as he
Walks along.

(Move arms and legs stiffly, remaining in same place.)

His head turns left,
His head turns right,
And both his eyes
Shine red and bright.

(Continue walking motions. Add head movement, left and right, then open eyes wide.)

Press this button;
He will say,
"How are all
My friends today?

(Stop all movement. Press button. Continue head movement, then speak in low voice.)

---

*"The Robot" from *My Big Book of Fingerplays* by Daphne Hogstrom. Copyright © 1974 by Western Publishing Company, Inc. Reprinted by permission.

Pull this handle;
He will tell:
"I am felling
Very well!"

(Stop all movement. Pull handle. Add head movement, low
voice.)

Book Talk

No More Monsters for Me by Peggy Parrish. il. by Marc Simont. New York:
Harper & Row, 1981.
   Introduce the story: "Minn has a problem. Her mom says she can't have a
pet. But when Minn finds a baby monster, she brings it home because her mom
didn't say anything about monsters. Now, what will Minn feed the monster?
Where will she hide it? What will Minn tell her mom that noise is in the base-
ment? And what will Minn do as the monster grows bigger and bigger?"

Applelard & Liverwurst by Mercer Mayer. il. by Steven Kellogg. New York:
Four Winds Press, 1978.
   Introduce the story: "Applelard enjoys a quiet and slow life with his
animals until he discovers a strange creature in his cellar. The creature is called
a rhinosterwurst, and Applelard names it Liverwurst. Liverwurst is very helpful and friendly until market day arrives, and then things get wild — all because
of some mushrooms that Liverwurst smells."

The Funny Little Woman by Arlene Mosel. il. by Blair Lent. New York: E. P.
Dutton, 1972.
   Introduce the story: "Meet the funny little woman. Her rice dumpling
rolls down a hole in the ground. When the funny little woman tries to get the
dumpling back, down, down she goes until she's underground in a strange
land. There she is captured by an unusual creature, a wicked one-eyed oni. The
wicked oni forces the funny little woman to make rice dumplings for all the
oni. That's all she does all day long. The funny little woman would rather go
home, but can she escape from the wicked oni?"

Participation Activity

"Creature Feature." Developed by the staff of the Thomas Crane Public
Library, Quincy, Massachusetts.
   Do Ahead: Make several odd-shaped heads out of different-colored
pieces of felt. Design and cut out features — eyes, ears, mouths, noses, and
antennae. Make them colorful and unusual.
   During the Program: Demonstrate how to compose a "strange creature."
Then either invite each child in turn to create a monster, or (and this has
worked more successfully) have each child add a feature until a monster is
created.

Ask the children to name the creature. Have them answer questions about the monster: Where does it come from? What does it do all day long? What does it eat? What does it do for fun? What would you do if you met this creature? What is its family like? Children love to create a whole profile of the creature. These questions also help to hold the attention of the children who are not busy creating the monster at that moment.

TRY THIS!

Read Aloud

Crowe, Robert L. **Clyde Monster**. il. by Kay Chorao. New York: E. P. Dutton, 1976.

Gackenbach, Dick. **Annie and the Mud Monster**. il. by author. New York: Lothrop, Lee & Shepard Books, 1982.

Galdone, Paul. **The Monster and the Tailor: A Ghost Story**. il. by author. New York: Ticknor & Fields/Houghton Mifflin, 1982.

Hutchins, Pat. **The Very Worst Monster**. il. by author. New York: Greenwillow Books, 1985.

Kellogg, Steven. **The Mysterious Tadpole**. il. by author. New York: Dial Press, 1977.

Stevenson, James. **What's under My Bed?** il. by author. New York: Greenwillow Books, 1983.

Watson, Pauline. **Wriggles: The Little Wishing Pig**. il. by Paul Galdone. New York: The Seabury Press, 1978.

Zemach, Harve. **The Judge: An Untrue Tale**. il. by Margot Zemach. New York: Farrar, Straus and Giroux, 1969.

Book Talk

Francis, Anna B. **Pleasant Dreams**. il. by author. New York: Holt, Rinehart and Winston, 1983. (This is a wordless book.)

Kellogg, Steven. **Mystery Beast of Ostergeest**. il. by author. New York: Dial Press, 1971.

Krahn, Fernando. **The Creepy Thing**. il. by author. New York: Ticknor & Fields/Houghton Mifflin, 1982. (This is a wordless book.)

Mayer, Mercer. **Liverwurst Is Missing**. il. by Steven Kellogg. New York: Four Winds Press, 1981.

Noble, Trinka H. **The Day Jimmy's Boa Ate the Wash**. il. by Steven Kellogg. New York: Dial Press, 1980.

Pinkwater, Daniel M. **Pickle Creature**. il. by author. New York: Four Winds Press, 1979.

Fingerplay and Action Rhyme

"Monsters," p. 64 in **Ring a Ring O' Roses: Stories, Games and Finger Plays for Pre-School Children**, rev. ed. Flint, Mich.: Flint Public Library, 1981. (This is a good accompaniment to *Harry and the Terrible Whatzit*.)

Filmstrip

Alligators All Around by Maurice Sendak. il. by author. Weston, Conn.: Weston Woods, 1976. 4 min. 20 sec.

Where the Wild Things Are by Maurice Sendak. il. by author. Weston, Conn.: Weston Woods, n.d. 4 min. 30 sec.

Piggies

PUBLICITY

A large pig graces your bulletin board with program information printed on its side. Also use a pig in profile on posters and handouts.

PROGRAM PLAN

Do you have a stuffed toy pig you can use as a mascot for your program?

Tell the children that you'd like to share some stories and books with them about an animal who is pink and fat, who likes to roll in the mud, and who has a curly tail—the pig.

Read Aloud

The Three Little Pigs by Paul Galdone. il. by author. New York: The Seabury Press, 1970.

Introduce the story: "You might have heard this story before. Let's find out what happens when mother pig sends her three children off into the world."

You might want to invite the children to join in on the refrain by the wolf.

Read Aloud

Yummers by James Marshall. il. by author. Boston: Houghton Mifflin, 1973.

Introduce the story: "Meet Emily and Eugene. They're going for a walk. You see, Emily is rather plump, and she needs to lose some weight. She thinks that exercise might help. But watch what Emily does on her walk. Can she get thin this way?"

Fingerplay

"Two Mother Pigs," p. 23 in **Ring a Ring O' Roses: Stories, Games and Finger Plays for Pre-School Children**, rev. ed. Flint, Mich.: Flint Public Library, 1981.

Introduce the fingerplay: "Let's share a story about ten pigs."

This fingerplay can be used with a large seated group. Show the children how the fingerplay is done, and then invite the children to do it with you. Try it again. (Text of fingerplay is in "Down on the Farm.")

Read Aloud

Mrs. Pig's Bulk Buy by Mary Rayner. il. by author. New York: Atheneum, 1981.

Introduce the story: "According to this story, pigs weren't always pink. They used to be white. This is the tale of how and why they changed color."

Fingerplay-Song

"This Little Pig," p. 23 in **Ring a Ring O' Roses: Stories, Games and Finger Plays for Pre-School Children**, rev. ed. Flint, Mich.: Flint Public Library, 1981.

Introduce the fingerplay-song: "Let's share a story about five pigs."

This is a very simple counting rhyme that can be used with any number of children. It's a satisfying hand rhyme because the action is easy, and children know or quickly learn the words. The song is found in:

Eye Winker, Tom Tinker, Chin Chopper by Tom Glazer. il. by Ron Himler. Garden City, N.Y.: Doubleday, 1973, pp. 80-81.

This Little Pig

This little pig went to market,   (Using forefinger of right
This little pig stayed home.   hand, touch thumb and
This little pig had roast beef,   fingers of left hand.)
This little pig had none,
This little pig cried, "Wee, wee, wee,
I can't find my way home."

Poetry

"To Market, to Market," in **This Little Pig-A-Wig and Other Rhymes about Pigs** compiled by Lenore Blegvad. il. by Erik Blegvad. New York: Atheneum, 1978.

Introduce the poem: "There are many rhymes about pigs in this book. I'd like to share one of them with you now."

Feel free to share other selections from this book, and don't forget to suggest that someone borrow the book and share it with someone at home.

Poetry

"There Was a Sad Pig with a Tail," p. 12, "There Was a Young Pig Who, in Bed," p. 30, and "There Was a Young Pig from Fort Wayne," p. 32 in **The Book of Pigericks** by Arnold Lobel. il. by author. New York: Harper & Row, 1983.

Introduce the poems: "Here's another book that has poems just about pigs. Take a good look at these silly pigs as I share a short story with you about each one."

These selections are appropriate to use with four and five year olds, although most of the other poems in this collection are best shared with older children.

Book Talk

Small Pig by Arnold Lobel. il. by author. New York: Harper & Row, 1969.

Introduce the story: "Small Pig is very upset. He liked life on the farm, and he especially liked his pigpen with its good, soft mud. But now the farmer's wife has decided to clean the farm—the farmhouse, the farm land, and the pigpen. Small Pig finds it too shiny and neat for him. He needs some nice mud. But where will he find it?"

Emmett's Pig by Mary Stolz. il. by Garth Williams. New York: Harper & Row, 1959.

Introduce the story: "Emmett lives in the city and has a room full of pigs—a pig bank, a stuffed pig, books about pigs, and glass pigs. But Emmett has never seen a real pig. He'd like to see one; he'd even like to have one in his room. His parents won't let him do that. But one day it's Emmett's birthday, and his parents tell him that one of his presents is in the country. Maybe Emmett's big wish will finally come true."

A Treeful of Pigs by Arnold Lobel. il. by Anita Lobel. New York: Greenwillow Books, 1979.

Introduce the story: "The farmer's wife really doesn't want to buy any pigs, but her husband tells her that keeping the pigs won't be a lot of work because they'll raise the pigs together. When the pigs arrive, however, the husband doesn't want to help at all. Will he help if the pigs fall like rain? No. Will he help if the pigs grow like flowers? No. Now what will his wife do to get him to keep his promise?"

Amanda Pig and Her Big Brother Oliver by Jean Van Leeuwen. il. by Ann Schweninger. New York: Dial Press, 1982.

Introduce the story: "Amanda wants to do things as well as her brother Oliver. She'd like to run, jump, and throw the way he does, but she can't. Amanda wants to tell a good secret and be Mighty Pig like Oliver, but she can't. Amanda learns, though, that there are things she can do best of all— better than even her brother Oliver."

TRY THIS!

Read Aloud

Gretz, Susanna. **It's Your Turn, Roger!** il. by author. New York: Dial Press, 1985.

Keller, Holly. **Geraldine's Blanket**. il. by author. New York: Greenwillow Books, 1984.

Marshall, James. **Portly McSwine**. il. by author. Boston: Houghton Mifflin, 1979.

McPhail, David. **Pig Pig and the Magic Photo Album**. il. by author. New York: E. P. Dutton, 1986.

McPhail, David. **Pig Pig Goes to Camp**. il. by author. New York: E. P. Dutton, 1983.

McPhail, David. **Pig Pig Grows Up**. il. by author. New York: E. P. Dutton, 1980.

McPhail, David. **Pig Pig Rides**. il. by author. New York: E. P. Dutton, 1982.

Rayner, Mary. **Garth Pig and the Ice Cream Lady**. il. by author. New York: Atheneum, 1977.

Steig, William. **Roland the Minstrel Pig**. il. by author. New York: Harper & Row, 1968.

Watson, Pauline. **Wriggles: The Little Wishing Pig**. il. by Paul Galdone. New York: The Seabury Press, 1978.

Zalben, Hilary. **Basil & Hilary**. il. by author. New York: Macmillan, 1975.

Book Talk

Brown, Marc, and Stephen Krensky. **Perfect Pigs: An Introduction to Manners**. Boston: Little, Brown, 1983.

Dubanevich, Arlene. **Pigs in Hiding**. il. by author. New York: Four Winds Press, 1983.

Galdone, Paul, reteller. **The Amazing Pig: An Old Hungarian Tale**. il. by Paul Galdone. Boston: Houghton Mifflin, 1981.

Jeschke, Susan. **Perfect the Pig**. il. by author. New York: Holt, Rinehart and Winston, 1980.

Lamont, Priscilla. **The Troublesome Pig: A Nursery Tale**. il. by author. New York: Crown, 1985.

Fingerplay and Action Rhyme

"Piggies" and "Piggy Wig and Piggy Wee," p. 4 in **Kidstuff**, vol. 2, no. 6, "Pig Pizzazz" edited by Sheila Debs. Lake Park, Fla.: GuideLines Press, 1983.

Song

"Pig Songs," pp. 8-9 in **Father Fox's Feast of Songs** with words and music by Clyde Watson. il. by Wendy Watson. New York: Philomel Books, 1983.

Film

Three Little Pigs. Burbank, Calif.: Walt Disney Company, 1933. 9 min.

Winter Tales

PUBLICITY

Use a snowman, a sled, a pair of ice skates, a pair of mittens, or a simple snowflake design on handouts and posters. Your bulletin board becomes a winter wonderland with children sledding, skating, and building snowmen. Fashion them out of construction paper. If you prefer, simply cover the board with snowflakes made out of tissue paper.

PROGRAM PLAN

Hang snowflakes from the ceiling, or tack them on a wall in the program area. Wear a scarf, a ski hat, and boots.

Introduction

Introduce the program: "Today, I'd like to share some stories with you about the winter. The winter is many things: snowy days, cold weather, red noses and cheeks, lots of fun. . . ."

Read Aloud

The Snowy Day by Ezra Jack Keats. il. by author. New York: Viking Press, 1962.

Introduce the story: "Winter is a fun time for Peter. His story might give you some ideas of things to do outside on a snowy day."

Read Aloud

The Mitten: An Old Ukranian Folktale retold by Alvin Tresselt. adapted from the version by E. Rachev. il. by Yaroslava. New York: Lothrop, Lee & Shepard Books, 1964.

Introduce the story: "Let's meet a young person for whom winter means trying to stay warm. That means collecting firewood and wearing warm woolen mittens. One day when he's out gathering firewood, the young boy sees something unusual happen. It almost seems like magic."

Fingerplay

"Snow Men," p. 48 in **Let's Do Fingerplays** by Marion F. Grayson. il. by Nancy Weyl. Washington, D.C.: Robert B. Luce, 1962.

Introduce the fingerplay: "In the story about Peter, one of the things he had fun doing was making a snowman with a smiling face. Well, I have a story about five snowmen that we can share."

Recite the rhyme, and then repeat it with the accompanying actions. Be sure to go through the many actions slowly for the children. Invite the children to join you, and then repeat this fun hand rhyme.

Snow Men*

Five little snow men
(Hold up one hand, fingers extended.)

Standing in a row,
Each with a hat
(Join thumbs and index fingers, and place on top of head.)

And a big red bow.
(Join thumbs and index fingers together to make bow under
    chin.)

Five little snow men
(Hold up one hand, fingers extended.)

Dressed for a show,
Now they are ready,
Where will they go?
Wait till the sun shines;
(Make circle with arms above head.)

Soon they will go
Down through the fields
(Bring arms down to lap.)

With the melting snow.

Read Aloud

Henry the Explorer by Mark Taylor. il. by Graham Booth. New York: Atheneum, 1966.

Introduce the story: "The winter can be a time for adventure, for discovering new things. And that's what Henry and his dog Angus like to do."

---

*From *Let's Do Fingerplays* by Marion F. Grayson. Copyright © 1962 by Robert B. Luce. Used by permission.

Book Talk

Bearymore by Don Freeman. il. by author. New York: Viking Press, 1976.

Introduce the story: "You probably noticed that although Henry thought he had seen a large bear, what he really saw were rocks that looked like a bear. The real bears were hibernating—asleep for the winter. Well, it's time for Bearymore to hibernate too. Unfortunately, hibernating is a problem for him this year. You see, Bearymore's boss at the circus tells him that everyone is tired of Bearymore's old tricks, and if he doesn't think of a new act, he'll lose his job. But if Bearymore has to sleep all winter long, when will he have time to think of a new circus act?"

Read Aloud

The Winter Picnic by Robert Welber. il. by Deborah Ray. New York: Pantheon Books, 1970.

Introduce the story: "Peter knows how to have fun outside on a snowy day and so does Adam. Adam would like his mother to join him too. Will she?"

Book Talk

The Self-Made Snowman by Fernando Krahn. il. by author. Philadelphia: J. B. Lippincott, 1974.

Introduce the story: "Peter had to make the snowman in his story, but here is a tale about a snowman who makes himself. It all begins when a ram kicks a snowball off a mountain, and the snowball grows bigger and bigger.

What's fun about this book is that it doesn't have any words. You can look at the pictures on each page and make up your own words to go with them."

City in the Winter by Eleanor Schick. il. by author. New York: Macmillan, 1970.

Introduce the story: "Jimmy spends a day at home when school is called off because of a blizzard. He learns that you can have fun indoors on a snowy day. Let Jimmy show you how."

Katy and the Big Snow by Virginia Lee Burton. il. by author. Boston: Houghton Mifflin, 1943, 1971.

Introduce the story: "Snow can create problems. Meet Katy, a red tractor with a big snowplow. Katy wasn't getting any jobs because there wasn't enough snow for her great big snowplow. But one day it snows and snows—ten inches of snow. All the regular snow trucks break down. No one can move, not the policemen or firemen or mailmen. This is Katy's big chance. Will she be able to rescue everyone and plow all the snow?"

Cross-Country Cat by Mary Calhoun. il. by Erick Ingraham. New York: William Morrow, 1979.

Introduce the story: "Snow can be a problem for animals too. Take Henry, for example. Henry is a most unusual cat—he can walk on his hind legs. This gives the boy who owns Henry an idea. He'll make a pair of skis for Henry the cat. Henry doesn't like this idea at all. But when the family leaves their mountain cabin, and Henry is left behind, Henry realizes that the only way for him to get back home is to use the skis he hates so much. Can Henry do it? Will he find his way back safely?"

Action Rhyme

Based on "Snowflakes," p. 48 in **Let's Do Fingerplays** by Marion F. Grayson. il. by Nancy Weyl. Washington, D.C.: Robert B. Luce, 1962.

Do Ahead: Cut snowflakes from tissue paper, crepe paper, or colored paper. Be sure to make extras.

During the Program: Use this activity with about twenty children, unless you have a lot of room for twirling bodies.

Introduce the program: "We've talked a lot about snowy days, and now it's time for us to share a story about snow and snowflakes."

Recite the short rhyme to the children, and then hand each child a snowflake. Keep one for yourself. I've invented several ways to act out this rhyme, and you can use one or all of these variations with the children:

1. Twirl the snowflake in your hand as you say the rhyme, and let it fall to the ground on the last line. Demonstrate and then invite the children to join you.

2. The children twirl with their snowflakes, and then *they* fall to the ground. Demonstrate this once, and then have the children try it a couple of times.

3. Form a big circle with the children. Twirl as a unit, and fall to the ground together.

Snowflakes*

(Flutter fingers high above head in the air, slowly falling to ground.)

Snowflakes whirling all around, all around, all around,
Snowflakes whirling all around
Until they cover all the ground.

---

*From *Let's Do Fingerplays* by Marion F. Grayson. Copyright © 1962 by Robert B. Luce. Used by permission.

Film

Six Penguins. New York: Contemporary Films, McGraw-Hill, 1971. 5 min.

Introduce the film: "Let's meet six penguins who love the cold weather because they can dance and have fun. However, they discover that there are dangers on the ice too."

Creative Dramatics

Act out **The Snowy Day** by Ezra Jack Keats.

Invite the children to become Peter and to do the things they saw him do when you shared the story with them earlier.

The children will remind you if you forget any of Peter's activities. Just in case, though, jot down each of Peter's adventures on a file card to which you can refer.

TRY THIS!

Read Aloud

Asch, Frank. **Mooncake**. il. by author. Englewood Cliffs, N.J.: Prentice-Hall, 1983.

Brenner, Barbara. **The Snow Parade**. il. by Mary Tara O'Keefe. New York: Crown, 1984.

Calhoun, Mary. **Hot-Air Henry**. il. by Erick Ingraham. New York: William Morrow, 1981.

Turkle, Brinton. **Thy Friend, Obadiah**. il. by author. New York: Viking Press, 1969.

Book Talk

Briggs, Raymond. **The Snowman**. il. by author. New York: Random House, 1978. (This is a wordless book.)

Hasler, Eveline. **Winter Magic**. il. by Michele Lemieux. New York: William Morrow, 1985.

Knotts, Howard. **The Winter Cat**. il. by author. New York: Harper & Row, 1972.

McCully, Emily Arnold. **First Snow**. il. by author. New York: Harper & Row, 1985. (This is a wordless book.)

Tresselt, Alvin. **White Snow, Bright Snow**. il. by Roger Duvoisin. New York: Lothrop, Lee & Shepard Books, 1947.

Other Story Forms

"The Snowstorm," pp. 13-14, and "The Snowman," pp. 26-27 in **Tell and Draw Stories** by Margaret J. Olson. Minneapolis, Minn.: Creative Story-time Press, 1963.

Poetry

Prelutsky, Jack. **It's Snowing! It's Snowing!** il. by Jeanne Titherington. New York: Greenwillow Books, 1984.

Fingerplay and Action Rhyme

"Five Little Snowmen" and "The Snowman," p. 25 in **Finger Plays That Motivate** by Don Peek. Minneapolis, Minn.: T. S. Denison, 1975.

"Gather Snow," p. 27 in **Finger Frolics: Over 250 Fingerplays for Young Children from 3 Years**, rev. ed. compiled by Liz Cromwell, Dixie Hibner, and John R. Faitel. il. by Joan Lockwood. Livonia, Mich.: Partner Press, 1983.

"I Am a Snowman" and "Let's Build a Snowman," p. 87, and "The Snowman," p. 91 in **Ring a Ring O' Roses: Stories, Games and Finger Plays for Pre-School Children**, rev. ed. Flint, Mich.: Flint Public Library, 1981.

Film

Grandfather's Mitten. New York: Phoenix Films & Video, 1974. 10 min.

Naughtiness

PUBLICITY

Take your cue from the books you'll be using for the program. Your visual for posters and the bulletin board can be Little Miss Muffet with the spider approaching her, the three little kittens who lost their mittens, or the monkeys from *Caps for Sale* with caps on their heads.

PROGRAM PLAN

Introduction

Introduce the program: "Are you ever naughty? Do you ever do things that your mom and dad don't want you to do? I bet most of the time you're good, and I'm sure you don't do the things that the animals and people do in the stories I have to share with you today."

Read Aloud

Tikki Tikki Tembo by Arlene Mosel. il. by Blair Lent. New York: Holt, Rinehart and Winston, 1968.

Introduce the story: "The two brothers in this story are warned by their mother not to play near the well. They disobey her and play near the well anyway. If your name is long like Tikki Tikki Tembo's, that's not a good idea!"

Read Aloud

Miss Nelson Is Missing! by Harry Allard. il. by James Marshall. Boston: Houghton Mifflin, 1977.

Introduce the story: "I'm sure that you don't act the way the children in Room 207 do. They're always misbehaving and being just awful to their sweet teacher Miss Nelson. Will they continue to be bad when Miss Nelson disappears?"

Book Talk

Miss Nelson Is Back! by Harry Allard. il. by James Marshall. Boston: Houghton Mifflin, 1982.

Introduce the story: "Miss Nelson has to have her tonsils out, so she won't be in school all week. The children in class 207 think it will be great—they can act up and be bad. But a youngster in Miss Nelson's class from last year warns that the children will probably get Miss Viola Swamp as their teacher. Instead, they get the principal, but he's almost as bad as Miss Swamp; he's so boring. The children decide to do something about him. When Miss Nelson hears what they're up to, it's time for her to take action."

Fingerplay

"Little Miss Muffet," p. 96 in **Finger Frolics: Over 250 Fingerplays for Young Children from 3 Years**, rev. ed. compiled by Liz Cromwell, Dixie Hibner, and John R. Faitel. il. by Joan Lockwood. Livonia, Mich.: Partner Press, 1983.
Introduce the fingerplay: "Let's meet a naughty creature—a spider."
Several actions accompany this rhyme, so share it with the children a few times after you've demonstrated it.

Little Miss Muffet*

Little Miss Muffet sat on a tuffet
(Make fist with thumb standing.)

Eating her curds and whey,
(Pretend to eat.)

Along came a spider
(Make running motion with fingers.)

And sat down beside her.
("Spider" sits down beside "tuffet.")

And frightened Miss Muffet away.
(Throw hands out.)

Felt Board Story

Caps for Sale by Esphyr Slobodkina. il. by author. Reading, Mass.: W. R. Scott, 1947.
Introduce the story: "No one seems to like or want the caps that the peddler sells. No one that is until the peddler innocently naps under a large tree."

---

*From *Finger Frolics: Over 250 Fingerplays for Young Children from 3 Years*, rev. compiled by Liz Cromwell, Dixie Hibner, and John R. Faitel. Copyright © 1983 by Partner Press. Used by permission.

You need the following items made out of felt: two peddlers, one standing and one seated; a tree; several monkeys; one set of individual caps; one set of caps attached by color — four red, four blue, four brown, and four gray; and the sun.

If you don't feel comfortable doing this as a felt board story or you don't have time, share the book with the children.

Felt Board Story

The Gunniwolf by Wilhelmina Harper. il. by William Wiesner. New York: E. P. Dutton, 1967.

Introduce the story: "Like the brothers in *Tikki Tikki Tembo*, the little girl in this story doesn't obey her mother when she's told not to go into the jungle. The little girl doesn't listen to her mother even though there are dangers in the jungle."

For this story you need the following items made out of felt: a mother; a little girl; a house; a tree; a sleeping gunniwolf; a running gunniwolf; and several white, pink, and orange flowers.

Book Talk

Good as New by Barbara Douglass. il. by Patience Brewster. New York: Lothrop, Lee & Shepard Books, 1982.

Introduce the story: "Poor Grady! His cousin K.C. is very naughty. K.C. destroys Grady's teddy bear, the bear Grady loved so much. Is there any way Grady's bear can ever be the same again? And if Grady does get the bear fixed, will he be able to keep his cousin K.C. away from it?"

Timothy Goes to School by Rosemary Wells. il. by author. New York: Dial Press, 1981.

Introduce the story: "Timothy is so excited about starting school. But there's this one kid at school, Claude, who's a real pain. Claude doesn't try to be friendly with Timothy. He just acts perfect, and he picks on Timothy. Claude is ruining things for Timothy — until Timothy meets Violet."

A Crocodile's Tale: A Philippine Folk Story by Jose Aruego and Ariane Dewey. New York: Scribner's, 1972.

Introduce the story: "This is not a very nice crocodile. A young boy just saved his life, and crocodile wants to thank the boy by eating him. The boy doesn't think that is fair, so he asks a basket, a hat, and a monkey what they think the crocodile should do. What will their answers be? Will they be able to help the boy out of his predicament?"

Rotten Ralph by Jack Gantos, il. by author. Boston: Houghton Mifflin, 1976.

Introduce the story: "Ralph is a very naughty cat. I don't know how Sarah can love him. Could you love a cat who took a bite out of each of your cookies? What if he rode a bicycle through the house? I wonder if Sarah can find a way to make Ralph a better cat?"

Filmstrip

Benjamin & Tulip by Rosemary Wells. il. by author. Weston, Conn.: Weston Woods, 1975. 4 min.

Introduce the film: "Benjamin's mom wants him to go to the grocery store. Sounds easy enough. But Benjamin has to get by his cousin Tulip first, and that's not as easy as it sounds."

TRY THIS!

Read Aloud

DePaola, Tomie. **Strega Nona: An Old Tale Retold**. il. by author. Englewood Cliffs, N.J.: Prentice-Hall, 1975.

Flack, Marjorie. **The Story about Ping**. il. by Kurt Wiese. New York: Viking Press, 1933.

Galdone, Paul, reteller. **The Three Bears**. il. by author. New York: The Seabury Press, 1972.

Lobel, Arnold. **Prince Bertram the Bad**. il. by author. New York: Harper & Row, 1963.

McCloskey, Robert. **Blueberries for Sal**. il. by author. New York: Viking Press, 1948.

McPhail, David. **Andrew's Bath**. il. by author. Boston: Little, Brown, 1984.

Preston, Edna Mitchell. **Squawk to the Moon, Little Goose**. il. by Barbara Cooney. New York: Viking Press, 1974.

Rey, H. A. **Curious George**. il. by author. Boston: Houghton Mifflin, 1941. (There are many titles in this series.)

Sendak, Maurice. **Where the Wild Things Are**. il. by author. New York: Harper & Row, 1963.

Turkle, Brinton. **Thy Friend, Obadiah**. il. by author. New York: Viking Press, 1969.

Zion, Gene. **Harry the Dirty Dog**. il. by Margaret Bloy Graham. New York: Harper & Row, 1956.

Book Talk

Burningham, John. **The Shopping Basket**. il. by author. New York: Thomas Y. Crowell, 1980.

Chess, Victoria. **Alfred's Alphabet Walk**. il. by author. New York: Greenwillow Books, 1979.

Gantos, Jack. **Worse than Rotten Ralph**. il. by Nicole Rubel. Boston: Houghton Mifflin, 1978.

Parker, Nancy Winslow. **Poofy Loves Company**. il. by author. New York: Dodd, Mead, 1980.

Potter, Beatrix. **The Tale of Peter Rabbit**. il. by author. New York: Frederick Warne, 1904.

Schatell, Brian. **Farmer Goff and His Turkey Sam**. il. by author. Philadelphia: J. B. Lippincott, 1982.

The Three Little Kittens. il. by Lorinda Bryan Cauley. New York: Putnam, 1982.

Watson, Wendy. **Lollipop**. il. by author. New York: Thomas Y. Crowell, 1976.

Wells, Rosemary. **Noisy Nora**. il. by author. New York: Dial Press, 1973.

Poetry

"Three Little Kittens," pp. 52-53 in **Tomie dePaola's Mother Goose**. il. by Tomie dePaola. New York: Putnam, 1985.

Fingerplay and Action Rhyme

"Three Little Kittens," p. 39 in **Story Programs: A Source Book of Materials** by Carolyn Sue Peterson and Brenny Hall. Metuchen, N.J.: Scarecrow, 1980.

Song

"Little Miss Muffet," p. 40 in **Singing Bee! A Collection of Favorite Children's Songs** compiled by Jane Hart. il. by Anita Lobel. New York: Lothrop, Lee & Shepard Books, 1982.

Filmstrip

Noisy Nora by Rosemary Wells. il. by author. Weston, Conn.: Weston Woods, 1975. 10 min. 20 sec.

Film

Miss Nelson Is Missing. New York: Learning Corporation of America, 1979. 14 min.

Your
Highness
Stories about Royalty

PUBLICITY

An ornate crown graces your handouts and posters. Your bulletin board has pictures (from magazines) of the British royal family. If you'd rather, depict a royal procession on your bulletin board, with characters fashioned out of construction paper.

PROGRAM PLAN

Wear a long robe and a crown to set the scene for this program.

Introduction

Tell the children that you want to share stories with them about royal people—kings, queens, princes, princesses—who sometimes wear clothes like the ones you're wearing. Continue in this manner: "You probably know about one famous royal family—Prince Charles, Princess Diana, Prince William, and Prince Harry. (Show the children a picture of them. You'll find photos in newspapers, magazines, and books.) Royal people are found in real life and in stories too. Sometimes they are smart, sometimes silly, sometimes good, and sometimes bad. Let's meet some of them now."

Read Aloud

The King's Flower by Mitsumasa Anno. il. by author. Cleveland, Ohio: William Collins and World Publishing, 1979.
Introduce the story: "The king in this story likes everything he owns to be big, the biggest, and usually he gets what he wants. But maybe there's something he can't have made big. And maybe it isn't best to have everything the biggest. You decide."
Follow this story by asking the children what things they'd like to own in a giant size. Ask them if having something in a giant size would make it better and if they would want everything they have to be the biggest.

Read Aloud

Sven's Bridge by Anita Lobel. il. by author. New York: Harper & Row, 1965.
Introduce the story: "Let's meet another silly king. He doesn't want to have the biggest of everything. Oh, no. But like the king in our first story, this king likes to get what he wants. And he wants things to happen when he wants them to happen. If they don't, watch out!"

Action Rhyme

"Royal Duke of York," p. 35 in **Ring a Ring O' Roses: Stories, Games and Finger Plays for Pre-School Children**, rev. ed. Flint, Mich.: Flint Public Library, 1981.

Introduce the rhyme: "Let's share a story about a king. He's not silly or bad. He's a very sensible fellow."

Although this rhyme has few actions, they move quickly, so share this rhyme with the children several times to give them a chance to do it smoothly.

Royal Duke of York

The Royal Duke of York,
He had ten thousand men.
He walked them up the hill,   (Walk forward, then
And then, he walked them down   backward.)
    again.
When you're up—you're up,
When you're down—you're down.
And when you're only half-way up,
You're neither up nor down.

(Variations can be added: Skip, run, gallop, jump, etc., up
    the hill and back.)

Read Aloud

Prince Bertram the Bad by Arnold Lobel. il. by author. New York: Harper & Row, 1963.

Introduce the story: "Before a king becomes a king, he's a prince. Here's a prince who might never be king because he's so naughty. What kinds of bad things does he do? Will he ever be a nice prince? Let's find out."

Read Aloud

The Princess and the Pea by Hans Christian Andersen. il. by Paul Galdone. New York: The Seabury Press, 1978.

Introduce the story: "Let's meet another prince. This prince is not naughty like Bertram; he's very nice. But he has a problem. This prince would like to marry a princess, and he just can't seem to find the right one."

Book Talk

The Prince and the Pink Blanket by Barbara Brenner. il. by Nola Langer. New York: Four Winds Press, 1980.

Introduce the story: "The king is very upset! His son, Prince Hal the Second, runs about the castle with his blanket. The king doesn't think it's right—a prince with a blanket—so the king commands his son and all the children in the kingdom to give up their blankets. This upsets the children, especially Prince Hal. But wait, maybe Great Uncle Maurice can help put things right."

The Princess and Froggie by Harve Zemach and Kaethe Zemach. il. by Margot Zemach. New York: Farrar, Straus and Giroux, 1975.

Introduce the story: "In this story you'll meet a princess whose best friend is very unusual; he's a frog named Froggie. If the princess loses something or has any type of problem, Froggie helps her. It's a good thing, too, because the princess loses her ball in a pond, she loses her penny, and she finds a bird firmly perched on her father's head."

The Duchess Bakes a Cake by Virginia Kahl. il. by author. New York: Scribner's, 1955.

Introduce the story: "A duchess is a type of royal person too. Usually they're very busy, but one day the duchess is bored. She decides to bake a cake. She puts everything into the mix: lots of yeast to make it rise, flour, sugar, almonds, raisins, eggs, all sorts of berries, and spices. She stirs it, pokes it, pinches it, and then sits on it. And the cake rises and rises higher and higher until the duchess is way above the castle. How will she ever get down?"

The Knight and the Dragon by Tomie dePaola. il. by author. New York: Putnam, 1980.

Introduce the story: "A knight is a royal person too. The knight in this story knows that he's supposed to fight fire-breathing dragons. The dragon has always read about fighting knights who wear armor and ride horses. So the knight and the dragon prepare to fight. But when they meet, the event doesn't turn out the way either of them expected. Now what will they do?"

Klippity Klop by Ed Emberley. il. by author. Boston: Little, Brown, 1974.

Introduce the story: "The knight in this story has the same idea as the knight we just met. And this is the tale of his journey to a dragon's cave. Again, things turn out very differently from the way the knight expected."

Filmstrip

The King, the Mice and the Cheese by Nancy Gurney and Eric Gurney. il. by Eric Gurney. New York: Random House, n.d. 6 min. 30 sec.

Introduce the film: "The mice are driving the king crazy! They're eating all of his cheese. What will he do? Who can solve this problem? You'll be surprised when you find out."

TRY THIS!

Read Aloud

Andersen, Hans Christian. **The Emperor's New Clothes**. retold and il. by Nadine Bernard Westcott. Boston: Little, Brown, 1984.

De Regniers, Beatrice Schenk. **May I Bring a Friend?** il. by Beni Montresor. New York: Atheneum, 1964.

Domanska, Janina. **King Krakus and the Dragon**. il. by author. New York: Greenwillow Books, 1979.

Galdone, Paul. **Puss in Boots**. il. by author. New York: The Seabury Press, 1976.

Noble, Trinka Hakes. **The King's Tea**. il. by author. New York: Dial Press, 1979.

Peet, Bill. **Cowardly Clyde**. il. by author. Boston: Houghton Mifflin, 1979.

Schwartz, Amy. **Her Majesty, Aunt Essie**. il. by author. Scarsdale, N.Y.: Bradbury Press, 1984.

Shulevitz, Uri. **One Monday Morning**. il. by author. New York: Scribner's, 1967.

Book Talk

Andersen, Hans Christian. **The Emperor's New Clothes**. il. by Anne Rockwell. New York: Thomas Y. Crowell, 1982.

Brunhoff, Jean de. **The Story of Babar, the Little Elephant,** translated by Merle Haas. il. by author. New York: Random House, 1933.

Burningham, John. **Time to Get out of the Bath, Shirley**. il. by author. New York: Thomas Y. Crowell, 1978.

Galdone, Paul. **Cinderella**. il. by author. New York: McGraw-Hill, 1978.

Van Woerkom, Dorothy. **Queen That Couldn't Bake Gingerbread**. il. by Paul Galdone. New York: Alfred A. Knopf, 1975.

Other Story Forms

"Henry and Mary," p. 307 in **Handbook for Storytellers** by Caroline Feller
Bauer. Chicago: American Library Association, 1977. (This is a fold-and-
cut story.)

Poetry

"Sing a Song of Sixpence," p. 13, "Old King Cole," p. 37, and "The Queen of
Hearts," p. 83 in **Tomie dePaola's Mother Goose**. il. by Tomie dePaola.
New York: Putnam, 1985.

Fingerplay and Action Rhyme

"Sand Castles," p. 7 in **My Big Book of Fingerplays: A Fun-to-Say, Fun-to-
Play Collection** by Daphne Hogstrom. il. by Sally Augustiny. Racine,
Wis.: Western Publishing, 1974.

"Sing a Song of Sixpence," p. 55 in **Let's Do Fingerplays** by Marion F. Grayson. il. by Nancy Weyl. Washington, D.C.: Robert B. Luce, 1962.

Song

"Sing a Song of Sixpence," p. 30 in **Singing Bee! A Collection of Favorite Children's Songs** compiled by Jane Hart. il. by Anita Lobel. New York:
Lothrop, Lee & Shepard Books, 1982.

Filmstrip

May I Bring a Friend? by Beatrice Schenk de Regniers. il. by Beni Montresor.
Weston, Conn.: Weston Woods, 1973. 6 min. 50 sec.

Film

The Tender Tale of Cinderella Penguin. New York: National Film Board of
Canada, 1981. 10 min.

Activities

Act out **Klippity Klop** by Ed Emberley. il. by author. Boston: Little, Brown,
1974.
    During this activity, you and the children pretend to ride a horse toward a
dragon's cave. Along the way, as you bob up and down, make the sounds that

the horse's hooves create on the different surfaces he travels. Say each sound long enough for the children to catch on and join you. Once you reach the dragon's cave and are scared by the dragon, gallop back home, and do the sounds the horse's hooves create in reverse. Repeat this activity if the children seem interested.

Jolly Giants

PUBLICITY

Tack two huge boots and the beginning of two large legs on your bulletin board. Use a giant or a beanstalk as the visual for your posters. The outline of a giant hand or foot encloses program information on your handouts.

PROGRAM PLAN

Set the mood by wearing huge clothes, oversized shoes, and a large hat.

Introduction

Introduce your program: "Like most types of people, there are good and bad and silly giants. Let's meet a few of them."

Read Aloud

The Little Hen and the Giant by Maria Polushkin. il. by Yuri Salzman. New
    York: Harper & Row, 1977.
    Introduce the story: "The little hen has put up with enough. The giant takes all of her eggs all the time. She might be a small hen, and he might be a huge giant, but hen is angry, and she's determined to make the giant stop stealing her eggs. Let's see what she does."

Read Aloud

The Runaway Giant by Adelaide Holl. il. by Mamoru Funai. New York:
    Lothrop, Lee & Shepard Books, 1967.
    Introduce the story: "Squirrel warns that there's a giant on the loose in the woods. But why does the giant appear to be different sizes to squirrel, bear, and rabbit? What kind of giant is he?" (It's actually a snowman that is melting.)

Action Rhyme

"Mr. Tall and Mr. Small," p. 54 in **Listen! And Help Tell the Story** by Bernice
    Wells Carlson. il. by Burmah Burris. Nashville, Tenn.: Abingdon, 1965.
    Introduce the rhyme: "Let's meet a very tall man—a giant—and a small man."

It's time for everyone to stand. The children remain in place for this activity, so you can certainly use this with a large group. Although the actions are easy, they do change rapidly, so demonstrate them first. Then do the rhyme slowly with the children. Repeat, doing it a bit faster.

Mr. Tall and Mr. Small*

There once was a man Who was tall, tall, tall. He had a friend	(Stand on tiptoes. Reach up as far as possible.)

Who was small, small,
   small.
	(Kneel and bend way
	   down.)

The man who was small Would try to call To the man who was tall,	(Cup hands near mouth. Look up.)
"Hello, up there!"	(Use high voice.)
The man who was tall At once would call	(Stand on tiptoes.)
To the man who was small, "Hello, down there."	(Bend from waist.) (Use deep voice.)
Then each tipped his hat And made this reply: "Good-bye, my friend."	(Stand straight.) (Tip an imaginary hat.) (Look up, speak in high voice.)
"Good-bye, good-bye."	(Bow, and speak in deep voice.)

Read Aloud

Jim and the Beanstalk by Raymond Briggs. il. by author. New York: Coward, McCann and Geoghegan, 1970.

Introduce the story: "Do you know the story of Jack and the beanstalk? Jack climbed that beanstalk and met the giant several times. Each time Jack outsmarted the giant and stole something valuable from him. Well, now it's Jim's turn to climb the beanstalk. He meets the giant's son. But the giant's son is nothing like the scary and mean giant his father was."

---

*From *Listen! And Help Tell the Story* by Bernice Wells Carlson. Copyright © 1965 by Abingdon Press. Used by permission.

Read Aloud

I Am a Giant by Ivan Sherman. il. by author. New York: Harcourt Brace
    Jovanovich, 1975.

Introduce the story: "What if you could be a giant? Would you be a mean
one like the giant in *The Little Hen and the Giant*? Would you be like *The
Runaway Giant*, very silly? Or would you be like the giant in *Jim and the
Beanstalk*, not very scary at all? What kinds of things would you do if you
were a giant? Before you tell me, listen to a few ideas from a little girl who
dreams about being a giant."

After the telling, invite the children to suggest what they'd do if they were
giants. What would be good about it? What would be bad about being a giant?

Book Talk

Gustav the Gourmet Giant by Lou Ann Gaeddert. il. by Steven Kellogg. New
    York: Dial Press, 1976.

Introduce the story: "Gustav is a very big eater like most giants. But
Gustav is also a very fussy eater. He eats only the finest foods, and he has only
the best cooks. All his food—strawberries, meats, cheeses—is stolen from
other people.

One day Gustav spies a lamb. Soon after, he learns about all the wonderful meals he can have with lamb. So Gustav steals the lamb from the young
boy who owns him. The boy doesn't like that at all, and he decides to trick the
giant and get his lamb back. But how will the boy outsmart the big, mean
giant?"

Mr. Tall & Mr. Small by Barbara Brenner. il. by Tomi Ungerer. Reading,
    Mass.: Addison-Wesley Publishing, 1966.

Introduce the story: "Mr. Tall is a giraffe. Mr. Small is a mouse. Giraffe
explains why it's wonderful to be tall. Mouse tells Giraffe all the advantages of
being small. But a crisis in the jungle shows Giraffe and Mouse how small and
tall are both wonderful ways to be."

The Giant's Feast by Max Bolliger. il. by Monica Laimgruber. Reading,
    Mass.: Addison-Wesley Publishing, 1976.

Introduce the story: "When big giant and little giant arrive at the giants'
feast, they learn that there's going to be a contest. Whoever can swallow the
biggest bit of food will be "King of the Feast." All the giants are excited! One
giant says he'll swallow a cake; another will swallow a pumpkin. Poor little
giant, how can he possibly compete? Maybe the apple in his pocket will give
him the answer."

TRY THIS!

Read Aloud

DePaola, Tomie, adapter. **The Mysterious Giant of Barletta: An Italian Folk-tale**. il. by Tomie dePaola. New York: Harcourt Brace Jovanovich, 1984.

Book Talk

De Regniers, Beatrice Schenk. **Jack and the Beanstalk; Retold in Verse for Boys & Girls to Read Themselves**. il. by author. New York: Atheneum, 1985.

Kahl, Virginia. **Giants, Indeed!** il. by author. New York: Scribner's, 1974.

Weisner, William. **Tops**. il. by author. New York: Viking Press, 1969.

Yolen, Jane. **The Giant's Farm**. il. by Tomie dePaola. New York: The Seabury Press, 1977.

Fingerplay and Action Rhyme

"Stilt Man," p. 50 in **Let's Do Fingerplays** by Marion F. Grayson. il. by Nancy Weyl. Washington, D.C.: Robert B. Luce, 1962.

"Suppose," p. 65 in **Ring a Ring O' Roses: Stories, Games and Finger Plays for Pre-School Children**, rev. ed. Flint, Mich.: Flint Public Library, 1981.

"Tall and Small," p. 98 in **Rhymes for Fingers and Flannelboards** by Louise Binder Scott and J. J. Thompson. il. by Jean Flowers. Minneapolis, Minn.: Webster Publishing/T. S. Denison, 1960.

Song

"The Friendly Giant," p. 176 in **Hap Palmer Favorites: Songs for Learning through Music and Movement** edited by Ronny S. Schiff. songs and activities by Hap Palmer. il. by Malinda Cowles. Sherman Oaks, Calif.: Alfred Publishing, 1981.

Squeakers!
Stories about Mice

PUBLICITY

Create your bookmark in the shape of a wedge of cheese, and design a mouse nibbling a piece of cheese for your handouts. For your bulletin board, create a scene depicting several mice running across a table and eating cakes, cheese, and cookies. Draw a grandfather clock with mice running up and down it on your posters.

PROGRAM PLAN

Read Aloud

Doctor De Soto by William Steig. il. by author. New York: Farrar, Straus and Giroux, 1982.

Introduce the story: "You have to be very careful about whose teeth you work on if you're a dentist who also happens to be a mouse. There are some animals, such as cats and wolves—you can think of others—who might not want to have you just look at their teeth."

Read Aloud

Alexander and the Wind-up Mouse by Leo Lionni. il. by author. New York: Pantheon Books, 1969.

Introduce the story: "Let's meet two mice who become good friends. Alexander is a real mouse. Willy is a toy wind-up mouse. At first Alexander thinks he'd like to be a toy mouse too. But is it really better to be a toy mouse? Let's find out."

Fingerplay

"Tiny Little Mouse," p. 4 in **Kidstuff**, vol. 2, no. 1, "Mice Are Nice!" edited by Sheila Debs. Lake Park, Fla.: GuideLines Press, 1982.

Introduce the fingerplay: "Let's share a rhyme about a very small and quiet mouse."

This fingerplay has several different motions, so recite and demonstrate twice before you invite the children to join you. Let the children do this several times.

Tiny Little Mouse

There's such a tiny little mouse,
(Hold thumb and forefinger close together to indicate size.)

Living safely in my house.
(Place right forefinger into clenched left fist.)

Out at night he'll creep, creep, creep
("Walk" fingers slowly up left arm.)

When everyone is fast asleep.
(Rest head on folded hands.)

But always in the light of day
(Put hands over head for sun.)

He'll softly, softly creep away.
(Creep fingers slowly back down left arm, and place in
    clenched left fist.)

Fingerplay

"Five Little Mice," p. 24 in **Ring a Ring O' Roses: Stories, Games and Finger
    Plays for Pre-School Children**, rev. ed. Flint, Mich.: Flint Public Library,
    1981.
    This is a short counting hand rhyme with actions that are easily seen by a
large group. Demonstrate and then invite everyone to join you. Share this a
couple of times. This fingerplay is also in:

Finger Rhymes by Marc Brown. il. by author. New York: E. P. Dutton, 1980,
    pp. 16-17.

Five Little Mice

(Hold up five fingers. Bend fingers down as verse
    progresses.)

Five little mice on the pantry floor;
This little mouse peeked behind the door;
This little mouse nibbled at the cake;
This little mouse not a sound did make;
This little mouse took a bite of cheese;
This little mouse heard the kitten sneeze.

"Ah-choo!" sneezed kitten, and "Squeak!" they cried,
As they found a hole and ran inside.
(Make running motions with fingers, and hide hands behind
     back.)

Read Aloud

Mouse Trouble by John Yeoman. il. by Quentin Blake. New York: Macmillan, 1972.

Introduce the story: "Take a windmill full of mice, add a miller who hates mice, and you have mouse trouble."

Book Talk

Amos and Boris by William Steig. il. by author. New York: Farrar, Straus and Giroux, 1971.

Introduce the story: "Amos is a mouse. Boris is a whale. How could a creature as small as Amos become friends with a huge whale? Well, one day Amos falls off the deck of his boat and into the sea. Boris rescues Amos and gives him a ride home on his back. The last thing Amos the mouse tells Boris is that if Boris ever needs help, Amos will help him. Boris laughs. How could a little mouse help a big whale? Little does Boris know, but the day will come when he does need Amos's help."

The Guard Mouse by Don Freeman. il. by author. New York: Viking Press, 1967.

Introduce the story: "Clyde is a guard mouse. His job is to make sure that small creatures don't slip through openings in the palace wall. One day some of Clyde's relatives come to visit him. He and his relatives decide to see the town of London—on a double-deck bus, on a rooftop, and from the top of a clock known as Big Ben. Then it's time to return to the palace. But where are the mice children who were left behind to take a nap in Clyde's furry hat?"

Frederick by Leo Lionni. il. by author. New York: Pantheon Books, 1967.

Introduce the story: "Winter is coming to this community of mice, and everyone is busy gathering corn, nuts, wheat, and straw. Everyone, that is, except Frederick. Frederick decides to catch the sun's rays and to gather colors and words. Everyone laughs at him. But when all the animals go to a cave for the winter and time passes, they learn that Frederick wasn't wasting his time."

Bravo, Ernest & Celestine! by Gabrielle Vincent. il. by author. New York: Greenwillow Books, 1982.

Introduce the story: "Meet Ernest the bear and Celestine the mouse. They have a problem. Their roof leaks, and they don't have the money to repair it.

But Celestine is a clever mouse, and she has an idea about how to raise money. Her idea involves a violin and some good songs. I hope it works."

Read Aloud

"The Wishing Well," pp. 8-16, and "The Old Mouse," pp. 48-54 in **Mouse Tales** by Arnold Lobel. il. by author. New York: Harper & Row, 1972.
   Introduce the story: "I'd like to share a story with you about a young mouse and a wishing well that says 'ouch.' "
   "I'd like to share another short story from this book about an old mouse and the embarrassing thing that happens to him one day."
   The illustrations in this book are rather small to share with a group, but the stories are so well written and humorous that the children will remain attentive while you read these selections. The same is true of all the stories in this book.

Action Rhyme-Song

"Hickory, Dickory, Dock," p. 94 in **Story Program: A Source Book of Materials** by Carolyn Sue Peterson and Brenny Hall. Metuchen, N.J.: Scarecrow, 1980.
   Introduce the rhyme-song: "Let's act out a rhyme about mice that I'm sure many of you have heard."
   Recite the rhyme while showing illustrations of the rhyme from your favorite Mother Goose collection, and then say the rhyme again with the accompanying actions. Invite the children to stand, and share this with them several times. Be sure that the children don't stand too close together because they'll be swinging their arms. The song is in:

Eye Winker, Tom Tinker, Chin Chopper by Tom Glazer. il. by Ron Himler. Garden City, N.Y.: Doubleday, 1973, p. 32.

Hickory, Dickory, Dock

Hickory, dickory, dock,
(Bend arm at elbow, holding up lower part for clock, palm
      open.)

The mouse ran up the clock;
(Use forefinger and middle finger of left hand for mouse.)

The clock struck one, and down he run.
(Clap hands for strike, then mouse runs down arm.)

Hickory, dickory, dock.

TRY THIS!

Read Aloud

Aesop. **The Town Mouse and the Country Mouse**. il. by Lorinda Bryan Cauley. New York: Putnam, 1984.

Aesop. **The Town Mouse and the Country Mouse**. il. by Paul Galdone. New York: McGraw-Hill, 1971.

Berson, Harold. **A Moose Is Not a Mouse**. il. by author. New York: Crown, 1975.

Gordon, Margaret. **The Supermarket Mice**. il. by author. New York: E. P. Dutton, 1984.

Holabird, Katharine. **Angelina and the Princess**. il. by Helen Craig. New York: Crown, 1984.

Holabird, Katharine. **Angelina at the Fair**. il. by Helen Craig. New York: Crown, 1985.

Holl, Adelaide. **Moon Mouse**. il. by Cyndy Szekeres. New York: Random House, 1969.

Kroll, Steven. **The Biggest Pumpkin Ever**. il. by Jean Bassett. New York: Holiday House, 1984.

Miller, Moira. **Oscar Mouse Finds a Home**. il. by Maria Majewska. New York: Dial Press, 1985.

Peppé, Rodney. **The Mice Who Lived in a Shoe**. New York: Lothrop, Lee & Shepard Books, 1981.

Book Talk

Freeman, Don. **Norman the Doorman**. il. by author. New York: Viking Press, 1959.

Gackenbach, Dick. **The Perfect Mouse**. il. by author. New York: Macmillan, 1984.

Ormondroyd, Edward. **Broderick**. il. by John Larrecq. Berkeley, Calif.: Parnassus Press, 1969.

Titus, Eve. **Anatole**. il. by Paul Galdone. New York: McGraw-Hill, 1957.

Vincent, Gabrielle. **Bravo, Ernest and Celestine!** il. by author. New York: Greenwillow Books, 1981.

Vincent, Gabrielle. **Ernest and Celestine's Picnic**. il. by author. New York: Greenwillow Books, 1982.

Wells, Rosemary. **Noisy Nora**. il. by author. New York: Dial Press, 1973.

Young, Miriam Burt. **The Sugar Mouse Cake**. il. by Margaret Bloy Graham. New York: Scribner's, 1964.

Other Story Forms

"How Mouse Became Small and Gray," pp. 43-47 in **More Tell and Draw Stories** by Margaret J. Olson. Minneapolis, Minn.: Arts & Crafts Unlimited, 1969.

Poetry

"The City Mouse and the Garden Mouse," by Christina Rossetti, p. 35, and "Mice" by Rose Fyleman, p. 36 in **A Child's First Book of Poems**. il. by Cyndy Szekeres. Racine, Wis.: Western Publishing, 1981.

Fingerplay and Action Rhyme

"The Baby Mice," pp. 15-15 in **Finger Rhymes** by Marc Brown. il. by author. New York: E. P. Dutton, 1980.

"This Little Mouse," p. 4 and "Cat & Mice," "The Field Mice," and "Five Baby Mice," p. 5 in **Kidstuff**, vol. 2, no. 1, "Mice Are Nice!" edited by Sheila Debs. Lake Park, Fla.: GuideLines Press, 1982.

Filmstrip

The King, the Mice and the Cheese by Nancy Gurney and Eric Gurney. il. by Eric Gurney. New York: Random House, n.d. 6 min. 30 sec.

Noisy Nora by Rosemary Wells. il. by author. Weston, Conn.: Weston Woods, 1975. 10 min. 20 sec.

Film

Doctor De Soto. Weston, Conn.: Weston Woods, 1984. 10 min.

Stories
Grandma Told
Folktales

PUBLICITY

What better symbol for folktales than Anansi, the spider. According to folklore, Anansi originally possessed all stories. Make Anansi out of colorful pieces of felt, and staple him to your bulletin board. Draw him on your handouts and posters too. For an example of what Anansi looks like, see *Handbook for Storytellers* by Caroline Feller Bauer. Chicago: American Library Association, 1977, p. 13.

PROGRAM PLAN

Introduction

Introduce the program: "Folktales are stories that have been with us for years and years. Your parents, your grandparents, people who lived long before you listened to these stories when they were children, and now you will hear some of them."

Read Aloud

The Cool Ride in the Sky by Diane Wolkstein. il. by Paul Galdone. New York: Alfred A. Knopf, 1973.
    Introduce the story: "We'll meet a tricky fellow in this story—a buzzard. He fools many of the animals in the hot desert sun, but he can't get away with his mischief forever. Or can he?"

Read Aloud

A Crocodile's Tale: A Philippine Folk Tale by Jose Aruego and Ariane Dewey. il. by authors. New York: Scribner's, 1972.
    Introduce the story: "Let's meet another tricky animal—a crocodile."

Fingerplay-Song

"This Old Man," pp. 68-69 in **Let's Do Fingerplays** by Marion F. Grayson. il. by Nancy Weyl. Washington, D.C.: Robert B. Luce, 1962.
    Introduce the fingerplay-song: "Just as there are stories that have been heard for many years, there are songs that people have sung through the years. They're called folk songs."

Say or sing the refrain of this fingerplay, and show the children the accompanying actions. Invite the children to try this part with you. Briefly go through the actions for each verse—you don't want the children to lose interest. Put all the actions and the words together, and have the children try it with you. They usually catch on right away. The song is in:

Eye Winker, Tom Tinker, Chin Chopper by Tom Glazer. il. by Ron Himler. Garden City, N.Y.: Doubleday, 1973, pp. 82-83.

This Old Man*

This old man, he played one,
(Hold up one finger.)

He played knick-knack on his thumb.
(Tap thumbs together.)

Knick-knack, paddy-whack, give a dog a bone,
(Tap knees, clap hands, extend one hand.)

This old man came rolling home.
(Roll hands.)

This old man, he played two,
(Hold up two fingers.)

He played knick-knack on his shoe.
(Tap shoe.)
(Repeat lines 3 and 4 above.)

This old man, he played three,
(Hold up three fingers.)

He played knick-knack on his knee.
(Tap knee.)
(Repeat lines 3 and 4 above.)

This old man, he played four,
(Hold up four fingers.)

---

*From *Let's Do Fingerplays* by Marion F. Grayson. Copyright © 1962 by Robert B. Luce. Used by permission.

He played knick-knack on the floor.
(Tap floor.)
(Repeat lines 3 and 4 above.)

This old man, he played five,
(Hold up five fingers.)

He played knick-knack on his drive.
(Tap floor.)
(Repeat lines 3 and 4 above.)

This old man, he played six,
(Hold up six fingers.)

He played knick-knack on his sticks.
(Tap index fingers.)
(Repeat lines 3 and 4 above.)

This old man, he played seven,
(Hold up seven fingers.)

He played knick-knack along to Devon.
(Point outward.)
(Repeat lines 3 and 4 above.)

This old man, he played eight,
(Hold up eight fingers.)

He played knick-knack on his pate.
(Tap head.)
(Repeat lines 3 and 4 above.)

This old man, he played nine,
(Hold up nine fingers.)

He played knick-knack on his spine.
(Tap spine.)
(Repeat lines 3 and 4 above.)

This old man, he played ten,
(Hold up ten fingers.)

He played knick-knack now and then.
(Clap hands.)
(Repeat lines 3 and 4 above.)

Read Aloud

The Funny Little Woman by Arlene Mosel. il. by Blair Lent. New York: E. P.
   Dutton, 1972.
   Introduce the story: "Let's meet a woman who likes to make rice
dumplings. She also likes to say "tee hee hee." Her cooking and her giggles get
her into trouble."

Read Aloud

The Tortoise's Tug of War retold by Giulio Maestro. il. by Giulio Maestro.
   Scarsdale, N.Y.: Bradbury Press, 1971.
   Introduce the story: "Ah, another trickster. This time it's a tortoise. This
huge turtle makes whale and tapir believe that they're playing tug-of-war with
him. But what is tortoise really doing? Watch!"

Book Talk

Two Greedy Bears: Adapted from a Hungarian Folk-Tale by Mirra Ginsburg.
   il. by Jose Aruego and Ariane Dewey. New York: Macmillan, 1976.
   Introduce the story: "What a problem! Two bears. Each wants to be the
thirstiest, the hungriest, the most tired. And so, of course, when the bears see a
piece of cheese and they decide to share it, it's almost impossible for them to be
fair about it. Instead, they end up getting what they deserve."

What's in Fox's Sack? An Old English Tale retold by Paul Galdone. il. by Paul
   Galdone. New York: Clarion Books, 1982.
   Introduce the story: "Fox is as tricky as buzzard, crocodile, and tortoise.
Fox leaves his sack with different people each time he goes to visit Squintum.
He tells each person not to look in the sack. Of course, each person does look,
and Fox is able to trade what was in the sack for something better. He trades
up from a bumblebee to a little boy. How long can fox get away with his
tricks?"

Millions of Cats by Wanda Gag. il. by author. New York: Coward, McCann
   and Geoghegan, 1928.
   Introduce the story: "In this story you'll meet a lonely man and woman.
They decide that a cat is just what they need to fill their home, so the man goes
in search of one. But what does he find? He not only finds one cat but trillions
of them covering a mountainside. How will he decide which cat to take home?"

Rum Pum Pum: A Folktale from India by Maggie Duff. il. by Jose Aruego
   and Ariane Dewey. New York: Macmillan, 1978.
   Introduce the story: "Magpie is very upset when the king takes his wife
and holds her prisoner. Magpie marches toward the castle to declare war on

the king. On his journey, he meets river, stick, the ants, and the cats. All of them are mad at the king for something the king did to them, and each of them proves very helpful to magpie when he's thrown into the king's prison."

Song

"Old MacDonald Had a Farm," pp. 56-57 in **Eye Winker, Tom Tinker, Chin Chopper** by Tom Glazer. il. by Ron Himler. Garden City, N.Y.: Doubleday, 1973.

Introduce the song: "Let's share another folk song that I'm sure most of you know."

After each verse, let the children supply the name of an animal for the next verse.

TRY THIS!

Read Aloud

Andersen, Hans Christian. **The Princess and the Pea**. il. by Paul Galdone. New York: The Seabury Press, 1978.

Asbjørnsen, P. C. **Three Billy Goats Gruff**. il. by Marcia Brown. New York: Harcourt Brace Jovanovich, 1957.

Asbjørnsen, P. C. **Three Billy Goats Gruff**. il. by Paul Galdone. New York: The Seabury Press, 1973.

Brown, Marcia. **The Bun: A Tale from Russia**. il. by author. New York: Harcourt Brace Jovanovich, 1972.

Elphinstone, Dayrell. **Why the Sun and the Moon Live in the Sky: An African Folktale**. il. by Blair Lent. Boston: Houghton Mifflin, 1968. (This adapts into a felt board story.)

Galdone, Paul, reteller. **Henny Penny**. il. by Paul Galdone. New York: The Seabury Press, 1968.

Galdone, Paul, reteller. **The Three Bears**. il. by author. New York: The Seabury Press, 1972.

Galdone, Paul, reteller. **Three Little Pigs**. il. by author. New York: The Seabury Press, 1972.

Galdone, Paul, reteller. **The Teeny-Tiny Woman: A Ghost Story**. il. by author. New York: Clarion Books, 1984.

Ginsburg, Mirra. **Mushroom in the Rain**. adapted from the Russian of V. Suteyev. il. by Jose Aruego and Ariane Dewey. New York: Macmillan, 1974.

Ginsburg, Mirra. **The Strongest One of All: Based on a Caucasian Folktale**. il. by Jose Aruego and Ariane Dewey. New York: Greenwillow Books, 1977.

Grimm, Jacob, and Wilhelm Grimm. **The Bremen Town Musicians**. retold and il. by Ilse Plume. Garden City, N.Y.: Doubleday, 1980.

Hogrogian, Nonny. **One Fine Day**. il. by author. New York: Macmillan, 1971.

Kent, Jack. **The Fat Cat: A Danish Folktale**. il. by author. New York: Parents Magazine Press, 1971.

Westwood, Jennifer. **Going to Squintum's: A Foxy Folktale**. il. by Fiona French. New York: Dial Press, 1985.

Zemach, Harve. **The Judge: An Untrue Tale**. il. by Margot Zemach. New York: Farrar, Straus and Giroux, 1969.

Zemach, Harve. **A Penny a Look: An Old Tale Retold**. il. by Margot Zemach. New York: Farrar, Straus and Giroux, 1971.

Fingerplay and Action Rhyme

"Eency Weency Spider," p. 31 in **Let's Do Fingerplays** by Marion F. Grayson. il. by Nancy Weyl. Washington, D.C.: Robert B. Luce, 1962.

"Hickory, Dickory, Dock," p. 94, and "I'm a Little Teapot," p. 99 in **Story Programs: A Source Book of Materials** by Carolyn Sue Peterson and Brenny Hall. Metuchen, N.J.: Scarecrow, 1980.

Song

See the list of songs in the last program plan, "Let's Make Music."

Filmstrip

A Penny a Look: An Old Story by Harve Zemach. il. by Margot Zemach. New York: Miller-Brody Productions, 1976. 5 min. 22 sec.

Why the Sun and the Moon Live in the Sky by Dayrell Elphinstone. il. by Blair Lent. New York: ACI Productions, 1973. 11 min.

Activities

Noah's Ark Dance-a-Story by Paul and Anne Barlin. il. by Zener Spector. Lexington, Mass.: Ginn & Co., 1964. (This is a creative dramatics activity in which the children are invited to create the ark — saw, hammer, and paint — and then become the animals who board the ark.)

Let's
Pretend

PUBLICITY

Ten fingers with faces and hats on them is an easy visual to create for posters, handouts, and bulletin boards.

PROGRAM PLAN

Introduction

Introduce the program: "Let's pretend; let's make believe. What do you like to pretend to be or do?" (Give some suggestions, and let the children offer their own ideas.)

Read Aloud

Henry Explores the Jungle by Mark Taylor. il. by Graham Booth. New York: Atheneum, 1968.
   Introduce the story: "Pretending is what Henry and his dog Laird Angus McAngus like to do the most. Today, they're going to explore the jungle, the impenetrable jungle. Remember, though, sometimes make-believe can become real."

Read Aloud

The Wedding Procession of the Rag Doll and the Broom Handle and Who Was in It by Carl Sandburg. il. by Harriet Pincus. New York: Harcourt Brace Jovanovich, 1922.
   Introduce the story: "I'm going to ask you to use your imagination for this story. In this wedding, a rag doll marries a broom handle. They have a wonderful wedding procession with some very interesting characters in it. Will you believe your eyes?"
   After the story, ask the children which wedding guests they liked the most — the chocolate chins; the dirty bibs; the tin pan bangers; or, perhaps, the musical soup eaters.

Fingerplay

"Ten Fingers," pp. 34-35 in **Listen! And Help Tell the Story** by Bernice Wells Carlson. il. by Burmah Burris. Nashville, Tenn.: Abingdon, 1965.

Introduce the fingerplay: "We use our imagination each time we pretend that our fingers become different things. This time our fingers will become ants, fish, and spiders!"

This works well with a large group. Demonstrate it once, and then invite the children to join you. Repeat.

Ten Fingers*

(Move fingers as action is described in verses.)

I have ten little fingers
With which I like to play.
They can be such different
    things
On any kind of day.

(Hold up hands with fingers spread apart.)

Now they're ten ants running
In the summer sun.
Hither, thither darting,
Work is never done.

(Move fingers lightly across table or lap.)

Now they're ten fish swimming
In a gurgling brook.
Safe from larger fishes,
Safe from any hook.

(Put palms together. Wiggle hands back and forth at wrist in swimming motion.)

Now they're spiders climbing
Up a silken line,
Safe in corners hiding
From your eyes and mine.

(Wiggle fingers as you raise arms.)

Now they are ten fingers
In a row like this.
They can help me clap my
    hands
And throw you a big kiss.

(Hold up hands with fingers spread apart.)
(Clap hands.)

(Throw kiss.)

(Say the next lines as quickly as you can.)

Ants running,

(Move fingers rapidly on table or lap.)

*From *Listen! And Help Tell the Story* by Bernice Wells Carlson. Copyright © 1965 by Abingdon Press. Used by permission.

Fish swimming,	(Make swimming motion with hands.)
Spiders climbing,	(Wiggle fingers as you raise arms.)
Hands clapping.	(Give two short claps.)
Bang! ·	(Give one big clap.)

Read Aloud

The Boy Who Was Followed Home by Margaret Mahy. il. by Steven Kellogg. New York: Franklin Watts, 1975.

Introduce the story: "In this story we'll meet a young boy who is followed home by an animal. It's not a cat or a dog. It's not a bird or a chicken. You'll be surprised when you see what it is." (The boy is followed by a hippopotamus.)

Book Talk

If I Had a Ship by Ben Schecter. il. by author. Garden City, N.Y.: Doubleday, 1970.

Introduce the story: "The young boy in this story has quite an imagination. He pretends to sail away from home on a ship. The little boy gathers presents to bring home, including a friendly giant, singing birds, chocolate candy, and a shiny gold crown. But the boy's mom doesn't care about these presents. There's just one thing she wants from her son."

Time to Get out of the Bath, Shirley by John Burningham. il. by author. New York: Thomas Y. Crowell, 1978.

Introduce the story: "Shirley's mom wants her to get out of the bath and dry off, but Shirley is busy. She's riding a horse, jousting with knights, visiting castles, and meeting kings and queens."

The Bed Book by Sylvia Plath. il. by Emily McCully. New York: Harper & Row, 1976.

Introduce the story: "Most of us sleep in ordinary beds, and a few of us have waterbeds, canopy beds, or bunk beds. But have you ever seen beds like these?"

Show the children various illustrations in the book, such as those of the inflatable bed, the elephant bed, the rocket bed, and the submarine bed. Give them time to respond to each illustration.

The Children's Dream Book by Walter Schmögner. text by Friedrich C. Heller. translated by Georgess McHargue. il. by Walter Schmögner. Garden City, N.Y.: Doubleday, 1972.

Introduce the story: "We all have dreams. Some dreams we remember; others we don't. Some of us have simple dreams and some of us have wild dreams, but have you ever dreamed about (show the corresponding illustrations from the book) an elephant who wears a watch on its leg? A lion that wears bows in his mane? A snail with a real house on its back? An octopus who wears shoes and smokes a pipe?"

Share other pictures from the book if the children enjoy these.

Fantastic Toys by Monika Beisner. il. by author. New York: Follett Publishing, 1975.

Introduce the story: "I'm sure that you have many toys at home, but you won't find any of these objects in your toy chest. Do you have (show the corresponding illustrations from the book) an animal umbrella that uses real animals? An automatic jump rope? Gigantic letters of the alphabet that are twice your size? An inflatable wall to draw on?"

Give the children time to respond to each picture, and share other illustrations from the book with them if they seem interested.

Participation Book

The Alphabeast Book: An Abecedarium by Dorothy Schmiderer. il. by author. New York: Holt, Rinehart and Winston, 1971.

Introduce the story: "Have you ever seen the letters of the alphabet turn into animals? You will right now."

Each letter turns into an animal whose name begins with the letter shown, and each letter transforms in three stages on a two-page spread. Cover the transformation with a piece of stiff board or paper, reveal slowly frame by frame, and let the children guess what animal the letter will become.

Try some of the easier letters first — B, butterfly; E, elephant; H, horse; Z, zebra — and then be more challenging — O, octopus, and U, unicorn.

Film

Harold's Fairy Tale. Weston, Conn.: Weston Woods, 1974. 8 min.

Introduce the film: "Harold draws himself into a garden, but an evil witch who lives there doesn't want Harold to grow anything in the garden. What will he do?"

TRY THIS!

Read Aloud

Christelow, Eileen. **Henry and the Dragon**. il. by author. New York: Ticknor & Fields/Houghton Mifflin, 1984.

Hazen, Barbara Shook. **The Gorilla Did It**. il. by Ray Cruz. New York: Atheneum, 1974.

Johnson, Crockett (David Johnson Leisk). **Harold and the Purple Crayon** by Crockett Johnson (pseud.). il. by author. New York: Harper & Row, 1955.

Keats, Ezra Jack. **Regards to the Man in the Moon**. il. by author. New York: Four Winds Press, 1981.

Lionni, Leo. **Let's Make Rabbits: A Fable**. il. by author. New York: Pantheon Books, 1982.

McPhail, David. **Pig Pig Rides**. il. by author. New York: E. P. Dutton, 1982.

Raskin, Ellen. **Who Said Sue, Said Whoo?** il. by author. New York: Atheneum, 1973.

Scheer, Julian. **Rain Makes Applesauce**. il. by Marvin Bileck. New York: Holiday House, 1964.

Schwartz, Amy. **Bea and Mr. Jones**. il. by author. Scarsdale, N.Y.: Bradbury Press, 1982.

Sendak, Maurice. **In the Night Kitchen**. il. by author. New York: Harper & Row, 1970.

Skorpen, Liesel Moak. **We Were Tired of Living in a House**. il. by Doris Burn. New York: Coward, McCann and Geoghegan, 1969.

Book Talk

Burningham, John. **Come Away from the Water, Shirley**. il. by author. New York: Thomas Y. Crowell, 1977.

Freeman, Don. **The Paper Party**. il. by author. New York: Viking Press, 1974.

Hutchins, Pat. **Changes, Changes**. il. by author. New York: Macmillan, 1970.

Johnson, Crockett (David Johnson Leisk). **A Picture for Harold's Room** by Crockett Johnson (pseud.). il. by author. New York: Harper & Row, 1960.

Keats, Ezra Jack. **The Trip**. il. by author. New York: Greenwillow Books, 1978.

Mayer, Mercer. **What Do You Do with a Kangaroo?** il. by author. New York: Four Winds Press, 1973.

McPhail, David. **Pig Pig and the Magic Photo Album**. il. by author. New York: E. P. Dutton, 1986.

Nerlove, Miriam. **I Made a Mistake**. il. by author. New York: Atheneum, 1985.

Noble, Trinka Hakes. **The Day Jimmy's Boa Ate the Wash**. il. by Steven Kellogg. New York: Dial Press, 1980.

Roche, Patricia K. **Webster & Arnold & the Giant Box**. il. by author. New York: Dial Press, 1980.

Schick, Eleanor. **Neighborhood Knight**. il. by author. New York: Greenwillow Books, 1976.

Wells, Rosemary. **Good Night, Fred**. il. by author. New York: Dial Press, 1981.

Wells, Rosemary. **A Lion for Lewis**. il. by author. New York: Dial Press, 1982.

Participation Book

(These books are imaginative and require use of the imagination.)

Emberley, Ed. **The Wizard of Op**. il. by author. Boston: Little, Brown, 1975.

Gardner, Beau. **Guess What?** graphics by author. New York: Lothrop, Lee & Shepard Books, 1985.

Gardner, Beau. **The Turn about, Think about, Look about Book**. graphics by author. New York: Lothrop, Lee & Shepard Books, 1980.

Hoban, Tana. **Look Again!** photos by author. New York: Macmillan, 1971.

Hoban, Tana. **Take Another Look**. photos by author. New York: Green-willow Books, 1981.

Wildsmith, Brian. **Puzzles**. il. by author. New York: Franklin Watts, 1971.

Fingerplay and Action Rhyme

"Look! I'm a Dragon," pp. 8-9 in **My Big Book of Fingerplays: A Fun-to-Say, Fun-to-Play Collection** by Daphne Hogstrom. il. by Sally Augustiny. Racine, Wis.: Western Publishing, 1974.

Filmstrip

Changes, Changes by Pat Hutchins. il. by author. Weston, Conn.: Weston Woods, 1973. 6 min.

It Looked Like Spilt Milk by Charles G. Shaw. il. by author. Weston, Conn.: Weston Woods, n.d. 2 min.

One Monday Morning by Uri Shulevitz. il. by author. Weston, Conn.: Weston Woods, 1972. 7 min.

Ten What? A Mystery Counting Book by Russell Hoban and Sylvie Selig. Weston, Conn.: Weston Woods, 1977. 4 min.

Film

Changes, Changes. Weston, Conn.: Weston Woods, 1973. 6 min.

Activities

"If I Were a Little Bird, High up in the Sky," p. 153 in **Games for the Very Young** compiled by Elizabeth Matterson. American Heritage Press/ McGraw-Hill, 1971. (The children pretend to be various creatures.)

"Let's Pretend," p. 60 in **Listen! And Help Tell the Story** by Bernice Wells Carlson. il. by Burmah Burris. Nashville, Tenn.: Abingdon, 1965. (The children pretend to be different animals and people.)

Magic to Do

PUBLICITY

Draw a magician's hat and a magic wand on your handouts and posters. Use the same visual on your bulletin board, but add a rabbit coming out of the hat. You might prefer to decorate your bulletin board with a three-dimensional hat and a trail of scarves or ribbons coming out of it.

PROGRAM PLAN

Introduction

Introduce the program: "Magic is fun, isn't it? You don't know what will happen next, and that's true of the stories I'd like to share with you today."

Read Aloud

Sylvester and the Magic Pebble by William Steig. il. by author. New York: Windmill Books, 1969.

Introduce the story: "Sylvester likes shiny stones, but would Sylvester, the donkey, know what to do if he found a magic stone or pebble? Would he use its magic wisely?"

Fingerplay

"Ten Fingers," pp. 34-35 in **Listen! And Help Tell the Story** by Bernice Wells Carlson. il. by Burmah Burris. Nashville, Tenn.: Abingdon, 1965.

Introduce the fingerplay: "Let's work some magic and turn our fingers into ants, fish, and spiders."

If you've used this fingerplay previously (in the program "Let's Pretend"), then you won't need to demonstrate again. Invite the children to share the rhyme with you, then repeat.

Read Aloud

Strega Nona: An Old Tale Retold by Tomie dePaola. il. by author. Englewood Cliffs, N.J.: Prentice-Hall, 1975.

Introduce the story: "Strega Nona is a witch, a good witch. Big Anthony is her helper, nosy and curious. Their quiet life turns topsy-turvy when Big Anthony disobeys Strega Nona and tries to dabble in her magic."

Book Talk

Big Anthony and the Magic Ring by Tomie dePaola. il. by author. New York:
　　Harcourt Brace Jovanovich, 1979.
　　Introduce the story: "You'd think that after Big Anthony's first experience
he'd never fool with Strega Nona's magic again, but Big Anthony didn't learn
his lesson. Anthony sees Strega Nona use a magic ring to make herself beautiful, and he decides to use the ring to make himself handsome. But when Big
Anthony wants to take the ring off, he can't. What will Anthony do when all
the girls in the town chase him and try to kiss him?"

Strega Nona's Magic Lesson by Tomie dePaola. il. by author. New York:
　　Harcourt Brace Jovanovich, 1982.
　　Introduce the story: "Big Anthony hasn't learned his lesson yet. Strega
Nona invites Bambolona, the baker's daughter, to stay with her and to learn
magic. Big Anthony wants to learn magic, too, but only girls can be Stregas.
That doesn't stop Big Anthony. He dresses up as a girl and goes back to Strega
Nona's. Anthony is a horrible student—he gets the magic all mixed up.
Anthony is headed for disaster unless Strega Nona can teach him a lesson,
fast."

Fingerplay

"Playmates," p. 54 in **Let's Do Fingerplays** by Marion F. Grayson. il. by
　　Nancy Weyl. Washington, D.C.: Robert B. Luce, 1962.
　　Introduce the fingerplay: "Let's work more magic on our fingers. We'll
turn our hands into children and houses."
　　Demonstrate this hand rhyme first, and then invite the children to join
you. Repeat.

Playmates*

A little boy lived in this house.
(Make fist with right hand, thumb hidden.)

A little girl lived in this house.
(Make fist with left hand, thumb hidden.)

The little boy came out of his house.
(Release right thumb.)

---

*From *Let's Do Fingerplays* by Marion F. Grayson. Copyright © 1962 by Robert B. Luce. Used by
permission.

He looked up and down the street.
(Move thumb slowly.)

He didn't see any one, so he went back into his house.
(Tuck thumb back into fist.)

The little girl came out of her house.
(Release left thumb.)

She looked up and down the street.
(Move thumb slowly.)

She didn't see anyone, so she went back into her house.
(Tuck thumb back into fist.)

The next day the little boy came out of his house and looked
    around.
(Release right thumb and move slowly.)

The little girl came out of her house and looked all around.
(Release left thumb and move slowly.)

They saw each other.
(Point thumbs toward each other.)

They walked across the street and shook hands.
(Move thumbs toward each other until they meet.)

Then the little boy went back into his house.
(Tuck right thumb back into fist.)

The little girl went back into her house.
(Tuck left thumb back into fist.)

Book Talk

The Magic Convention by Sandra Hochman. il. by Ben Shecter. Garden City,
    N.Y.: Doubleday, 1971.

Introduce the story: "Amanda has a wonderful time when she goes to a
magic convention with her Uncle Bill, a magician. Amanda sees amazing
tricks. One magician makes seven chickens come out of one egg. Another
magician does tricks with a magic umbrella, and a third magician does card
tricks. Amanda enjoys these acts and many others, too, and guess what
Amanda decides to be when she grows up?"

Brimhall Turns to Magic by Judy Delton. il. by Bruce Degen. New York: Lothrop, Lee & Shepard Books, 1979.

Introduce the story: "Brimhall the bear decides that he's going to be a magician. He gathers all the items he'll need—his magic hat, his magic wand, his cape—and, finally, he's ready. Brimhall is going to pull a rabbit out of a hat, and he does. How wonderful. But Brimhall can't make the rabbit disappear. What will he do with the rabbit?"

It's Magic? by Robert Lopshire. il. by author. New York: Macmillan, 1969.

Introduce the story: "You're never sure if the magic that Tad the bear does in this book will work or not. Some of the tricks are silly, some are jokes, some are barely tricks at all, and others are easy and fun to do. Try some of the tricks at home with the help of an older person. I especially like the magic clip trick and the magic star trick."

Demonstration

"Magic Tricks."

Introduce the demonstration: "We've talked a lot about magic, and now I'd like to share several magic tricks with you."

You'll want to have your tricks set up in advance. Use a table situated behind the children. Simply walk to the table, and ask the children to turn around and face you. Be sure the tricks are prepared in the order in which you plan to do them.

These tricks are easy to learn and to execute. They do not require a lot of preparation or coordination and they can be done by one person.

"Balloon in the Bag," pp. 10-11, and "Noodle's Cookies," pp. 34-35 in **Funny Magic: Easy Tricks for Young Magicians** by Rose Wyler and Gerald Ames. New York: Parents Magazine Press, 1972.

"Magic Clip" in **It's Magic?** by Robert Lopshire. il. by author. New York: Macmillan, 1969, unpaged.

"Rabbit in a Hat," pp. 33-34, "The Funny Paper Loops," pp. 48-49, "Impossible Trick," pp. 50-52, and "The Magic Cone," pp. 53-55 in **Give a Magic Show!** by Burton Marks and Rita Marks. il. by Don Madden. New York: Lothrop, Lee & Shepard Books, 1977.

"Spooky Hand," pp. 12-13, and "Candy for Willie," pp. 40-41 in **Spooky Tricks** by Rose Wyler and Gerald Ames. il. by Tālivaldis Stubis. New York: Harper & Row, 1968.

TRY THIS!

Read Aloud

Brown, Marc Tolon. **Arthur's April Fool**. il. by author. Boston: Little, Brown, 1983.

Freeman, Don. **The Paper Party**. il. by author. New York: Viking Press, 1974.

Galdone, Paul. **The Magic Porridge Pot**. il. by author. Boston: Houghton Mifflin, 1976.

Johnston, Tony. **The Witch's Hat**. il. by Margot Tomes. New York: Putnam, 1984.

Slobodkina, Louis. **Magic Michael**. il. by author. New York: Macmillan, 1944.

Book Talk

Alexander, Sue. **Marc the Magnificent**. il. by Tomie dePaola. New York: Pantheon Books, 1978.

Aliki. **The Wish Workers**. il. by author. New York: Dial Press, 1962.

Anderson, Lonzo, and Adrienne Adams. **Two Hundred Rabbits**. il. by Adrienne Adams. New York: Viking Press, 1968.

Freeman, Don. **The Chalk Box Story**. il. by author. Philadelphia: J. B. Lippincott, 1976.

Gagliardi, Maria Francesca. **The Magic Fish**. il. by Stepán Zavrel. New York: Putnam, 1966.

McDermott, Gerald. **The Magic Tree: A Tale from the Congo**. il. by author. New York: Holt, Rinehart and Winston, 1973.

Tresselt, Alvin. **The World in a Candy Egg**. il. by Roger Duvoisin. New York: Lothrop, Lee & Shepard Books, 1967.

Watson, Pauline. **Wriggles: The Wishing Pig**. il. by Paul Galdone. New York: The Seabury Press, 1978.

Filmstrip

Harold and the Purple Crayon by Crocket Johnson. il. by author. Weston, Conn.: Weston Woods, n.d. 7 min.

Film

Harold's Fairy Tale. Weston, Conn.: Weston Woods, 1973. 8 min.

The Sorcerer's Apprentice. Burbank, Calif.: Walt Disney Company, n.d. 10 min.

Activities

Magic tricks in **Magic Secrets** by Rose Wyler and Gerald Ames. il. by Tālivaldis Stubis. New York: Harper & Row, 1967.

Recite the chant from **Strega Nona** with the children. Be sure to use a small pot.

Let's
Make Music

PUBLICITY

Cover your bulletin board with a collage of musical instruments: violin, trumpet, drum, piano, guitar, harmonica, tuba, flute, cymbals, and triangle, for example. If you prefer, draw a large staff on your board, and tack musical notes on it. A horn heralds program information on your handouts, and any posters you make can be shaped like a drum, a record, or a guitar.

PROGRAM PLAN

Introduction

Introduce the program: "Music is all around us. Sometimes you hear people singing or whistling a song. Maybe someone you know plays the piano, a guitar, or some other instrument. You probably listen to records and cassettes, and maybe you listen to music on the radio. There are many stories about music and musicians too. I'd like to share some of them with you now."

Read Aloud

The Troll Music by Anita Lobel. il. by author. New York: Harper & Row, 1966.
Introduce the story: "The musicians in this story play beautiful music together until something unexpected happens to them." (The musicians offend a troll, and he changes their music into animal sounds.)

Read Aloud

The Bremen Town Musicians retold from Grimm by Ruth Belov Gross. il. by Jack Kent. New York: Scholastic Book Services, 1974.
Introduce the story: "A donkey, a dog, a cat, and a rooster plan to make music in Bremen Town until something unexpected happens to them too. They end up using their music in a different way from what they expected."

Fingerplay-Song

"Eency Weency Spider," p. 63 in **Ring a Ring O' Roses: Stories, Games and Finger Plays for Pre-School Children**, rev. ed. Flint, Mich.: Flint Public Library, 1981.
Introduce the fingerplay-song: "Let's make some music!"

Demonstrate the actions as you sing or chant this rhyme, and then try it with the children a couple of times. Many of the children are probably already familiar with the rhyme and the song. The song is in:

Eye Winker, Tom Tinker, Chin Chopper by Tom Glazer. il. by Ron Himler. Garden City, N.Y.: Doubleday, 1973, pp. 22-23.

Eency Weency Spider

An eency weency spider
Climbed up the water spout.
(One hand climbs up arm to shoulder.)

Down came the rain
(Raise hands high in air, and drop them down quickly.)

And washed the spider out.
(Hand slides down arm.)

Out came the sun
(Arms form circle over head.)

And dried up all the rain.
The eency, weency spider
Climbed up the spout again.
(Hand goes back up arm to shoulder.)

Action Rhyme-Song

"Teapot," pp. 26-27 in **Ring a Ring O' Roses: Stories, Games and Finger Plays for Pre-School Children**, rev. ed. Flint, Mich.: Flint Public Library, 1981.
Introduce the rhyme-song: "Let's make more music!"
Invite the children to sing and act out this rhyme a few times. (The text of the action rhyme is found in "Yummers: Stories about Food.") The song is in:

Eye Winker, Tom Tinker, Chin Chopper by Tom Glazer. il. by Ron Himler. Garden City, N.Y.: Doubleday, 1973, p. 36.

Read Aloud

Lentil by Robert McCloskey. il. by author. New York: Viking Press, 1940, 1968.
Introduce the story: "We sing and sound wonderful together, but what happens if you can't sing? How else can you make music? Let's see how a

young boy named Lentil solves this problem and how one day his solution comes in handy."

Book Talk

Roland, the Minstrel Pig by William Steig. il. by author. New York: Harper & Row, 1968.

Introduce the story: "Roland is a singing pig, and one day he decides to seek his fame and fortune in the world. Not long into his travels, Roland meets Sebastian, a wolf. Sebastian promises to take Roland to the palace where he can play for the king and perhaps become the king's musician. But Sebastian really has other ideas. He has his heart set on making a tasty meal out of Roland! Will Roland realize Sebastian's plan? Will he ever get to the king's palace? Have someone at home read this book to you, and you'll find out what happens."

Arthur's New Power by Russell C. Hoban. il. by author. New York: Thomas Y. Crowell, 1978.

Introduce the story: "It's time for the crocodile family to take drastic steps. Every time Arthur plugs in his electric guitar, all the electricity is sapped. This is the third time that Arthur has put the house in darkness. Father decides that the only way to use less electricity is to unplug everything, but Arthur has a better solution. He finds a way to make his own electricity. How does he do that?"

Max, the Music Maker by Miriam B. Stecher and Alice Kandell. photos by Alice Kandell. New York: Lothrop, Lee & Shepard Books, 1980.

Introduce the story: "Max hears music everywhere. He hears a cat purring, and he hears the train in the subway go 'bimble-dee-bim.' Max makes music too. He clicks a stick against a fence, he crashes pot lids together, and he uses other instruments too. Maybe Max will give you some ideas about how to make music."

Lizard's Song by George Shannon. il. by Jose Aruego and Ariane Dewey. New York: Greenwillow Books, 1981.

Introduce the story: "Lizard sings a wonderful song. Bear hears Lizard singing, and he wants the song to be his too. He demands that lizard teach it to him. But when Lizard shares the tune with him, Bear can't remember it. Bear is so unhappy, but lizard has an idea. He'll teach Bear a special song that Bear is sure to remember. Find out why."

The Farmer in the Dell. il. by Diane S. Zuromskiis. Boston: Little, Brown, 1978.

Introduce the story: "Many of you have probably heard this song before. But do you know what the farmer looks like? Or his wife? Do you know what kind of house they live in? Well, the person who drew the pictures for this book shows you how the farmer and his family look and just what happens on their farm."

London Bridge Is Falling Down: The Song and the Game. il. by Ed Emberley. Boston: Little, Brown, 1967.

Introduce the story: "London Bridge is falling down! How will it be built again? Wood or clay won't work. Iron bars will break. Gold and silver must be used and a guard hired so the gold and silver won't be stolen. But what if the guard falls asleep? Share this book with someone at home, and you'll find out all the problems there are in fixing London Bridge. Later, you can sing the song and play the game at home too."

Song

"Old MacDonald Had a Farm," p. 56 in **Eye Winker, Tom Tinker, Chin Chopper** by Tom Glazer. il. by Ron Himler. Garden City, N.Y.: Doubleday, 1973.

Introduce the song: "Let's sing a song that I'm sure everyone knows by now."

Share this song, and try to think of some animals that you might not have used before in other programs.

Film

Foolish Frog. Weston, Conn.: Weston Woods, 1972. 9 min.

Introduce the film: "Let's find out how a whole town of people, animals, barns, grass, and water could go wild because of a song about a frog."

TRY THIS!

Read Aloud

Harper, Wilhelmina. **The Gunniwolf**. il. by William Wiesner. New York: E. P. Dutton, 1967.

Isadora, Rachel. **Ben's Trumpet**. il. by author. New York: Greenwillow Books, 1979.

Keats, Ezra Jack. **Apt. 3**. il. by author. New York: Macmillan, 1971.

McCrady, Lady. **Junior's Tune**. il. by author. New York: Holiday House, 1980.

Shannon, George. **Dance Away**. il. by Jose Aruego and Ariane Dewey. New York: Greenwillow Books, 1982.

Wolkstein, Diane. **The Banza: A Haitian Story**. il. by Marc Brown. New York: Dial Press, 1981.

Book Talk

Caseley, Judith. **Molly Pink**. il. by author. New York: Greenwillow Books, 1985.

Hurd, Thatcher. **Mama Don't Allow**. il. by author. New York: Harper & Row, 1984.

Lionni, Leo. **Geraldine, the Music Mouse**. il. by author. New York: Pantheon Books, 1979.

Vincent, Gabrielle. **Bravo, Ernest and Celestine**. il. by author. New York: Greenwillow Books, 1981.

Williams, Vera B. **Music, Music for Everyone**. New York: Greenwillow Books, 1984.

Zion, Gene. **Harry and the Lady Next Door**. il. by Margaret Bloy Graham. New York: Harper & Row, 1960.

Fingerplay and Action Rhyme

"The Finger Band," p. 37, and "Drums," p. 79 in **Ring a Ring O' Roses: Stories, Games and Finger Plays for Pre-School Children**, rev. ed. Flint, Mich.: Flint Public Library, 1981.

"I Am a Fine Musician," p. 87 in **Let's Do Fingerplays** by Marion F. Grayson. il. by Nancy Weyl. Washington, D.C.: Robert B. Luce, 1962.

"If I Could Play," p. 12 in **Finger Frolics: Over 250 Fingerplays for Young Children from 3 Years**, rev. ed. compiled by Liz Cromwell, Dixie Hibner, and John R. Faitel. il. by Joan Lockwood. Livonia, Mich.: Partner Press, 1983.

"The Young Musician," p. 90 in **Listen! And Help Tell the Story** by Bernice Wells Carlson. il. by Burmah Burris. Nashville, Tenn.: Abingdon, 1965.

Song

The Farmer in the Dell. il. by Diane Stanley. Boston: Little, Brown, 1978.

Hush Little Baby. il. by Margot Zemach. New York: E. P. Dutton, 1976.

"Hush Little Baby," p. 33, "I Know an Old Lady," pp. 34-35, "The Musicians," pp. 52-55, and "This Old Man," pp. 82-83 in **Eye Winker, Tom Tinker, Chin Chopper** by Tom Glazer. il. by Ron Himler. Garden City, N.Y.: Doubleday, 1973.

Langstaff, John. **Oh, A-Hunting We Will Go**. il. by Nancy Winslow Parker. New York: Atheneum, 1974.

London Bridge Is Falling Down. il. by Peter Spier. Garden City, N.Y.: Doubleday, 1967.

Seeger, Pete, and Charles Seeger. **The Foolish Frog**. music adapted from an old song. book adapted and designed from Firebird Film by Gene Deitch. il. by Miloslav Jagr. New York: Macmillan, 1973.

Westcott, Nadine. **I Know an Old Lady Who Swallowed a Fly**. il. by author. Boston: Little, Brown, 1980.

Film

Drummer Hoff. Weston, Conn.: Weston Woods, 1969. 5 min.

I Know an Old Lady Who Swallowed a Fly. Chicago: International Film Bureau, 1966. 6 min.

The Mole and the Music. New York: Phoenix Films & Video, 1976. 6 min.

Resources
and Aids

A selective list of books and periodicals that have proved useful in planning and executing picture book story hours.

Bauer, Caroline. **Handbook for Storytellers**. Chicago: American Library Association, 1977.

Bauer's handbook is chock-full of ideas for planning, publicizing, and executing programs for children of all ages, especially elementary level. Part Three is particularly useful in planning story hours for preschoolers. You'll find fairly comprehensive how-to's on making and presenting board stories — chalk, felt, and magnetic. If you plan to make and use puppets or to do creative dramatics and fold-and-cut stories in your programs, refer to this book. There are also bibliographies throughout the text that direct you to other detailed books written on a particular type of activity.

Brown, Marc. **Finger Rhymes**. il. by author. New York: E. P. Dutton, 1980.

Brown, Marc. **Hand Rhymes**. il. by author. New York: E. P. Dutton, 1985.

These two small collections of fingerplays contain old favorites and some less familiar rhymes. Subjects include animals, holidays, and the seasons. Each rhyme has instructions for use as a fingerplay in the form of easy-to-follow diagrams. What distinguishes these collections are the double-page illustrations that compliment each rhyme. They are whimsical, detailed black-and-white drawings that are perfect to show to a group of children when you read each rhyme aloud.

Carlson, Bernice Wells. **Listen! And Help Tell the Story**. il. by Burmah Burris. Nashville, Tenn.: Abingdon, 1965.

You'll refer again and again to this original, clever, and varied collection of well-written fingerplays, action verses, and poems with sound effects. These activities cover a variety of subjects from bees and penguins to robots and Halloween. There are nineteen fingerplays, with easy and clear directions that appear next to the line to which they refer. You'll want to use all of them, and you'll want to try the fourteen action verses that are also appropriate for four and five year olds. Many of the poems with sound effects can be shared with this age group too. The other material — action stories, stories with sound effects, poems with refrains, and poems with choruses — is best used with older children.

Cromwell, Liz, Dixie Hibner, and John R. Faitel, comps. **Finger Frolics: Over 250 Fingerplays for Children from 3 Years**, rev. ed. il. by Joan Lockwood. Livonia, Mich.: Partner Press, 1983.

What distinguishes the fingerplays in this large spiral-bound paperback from others is their contemporary sound. The language is not formal or dated, which is a drawback of some fingerplays. Many of the rhymes in this collection are meant to be instructive, and they are perhaps best used in a school rather than a library setting. The table of contents quickly leads you to poems and rhymes about home, seasons, animals, weather, and holidays, among other subjects.

Debs, Sheila, ed. **Kidstuff: A Treasury of Early Childhood Enrichment Materials**. Lake Park, Fla.: GuideLines Press, Nov. 1981- .

Kidstuff describes itself as a "monthly by-mail treasury of programming ideas." Each multipaged pamphlet contains new and original material, as well as material from other sources, on one subject. Subjects have included families, babies, friendship, lions, insects, and homes. The material is aimed at toddlers, preschoolers, and primary grade children.

In particular, check out the ideas for flannel board stories, creative dramatics, and puppet plays. You'll find clear, direct instructions and patterns to make and use puppets and flannel board characters. Craft and activity ideas are well thought out, although some of them might be too time consuming for your story program.

Glazer, Tom. **Do Your Ears Hang Low? Fifty More Musical Fingerplays**. il. by Mila Lazarevich. Garden City, N.Y.: Doubleday, 1980.

Glazer, Tom. **Eye Winker, Tom Tinker, Chin Chopper**. il. by Ron Himler. Garden City, N.Y.: Doubleday, 1973.

Eye Winker, Tom Tinker, Chin Chopper is a delightful, illustrated collection that includes fifty familiar and unfamiliar musical fingerplays. Although piano arrangements and guitar chords are included, the songs with all their verses can be sung without accompaniment. The fingerplays can also be enjoyed by themselves. The author has included extremely explicit and lucid instructions for using them. You will not have to struggle to learn these fingerplays, and most are easy enough for preschoolers to execute. Use "This Old Man" in a folktale program or "The Bear Went over the Mountain" in a program on bears, for example.

Do Your Ears Hang Low? is the companion book to Eye Winker, and it shares the same excellent qualities. In it you can find other favorite song-fingerplays, including "Little Jack Horner," "London Bridge Is Falling Down," "Over in the Meadow," and "Ten in a Bed."

Grayson, Marion F. **Let's Do Fingerplays**. il. by Nancy Weyl. Washington, D.C.: Robert B. Luce, 1962.

Some of the fingerplays in this book are dated, but most of them are still enjoyed by four and five year olds. "The World Outdoors" is a short section, but the fingerplays on the seasons are quite good. The collection is also strong on Christmas and Halloween fingerplays and counting rhymes. Instructions for the actions follow each line of verse.

Hart, Jane, comp. **Singing Bee! A Collection of Favorite Children's Songs**. il. by Anita Lobel. New York: Lothrop, Lee & Shepard Books, 1982.

Lullabies, Mother Goose rhymes, fingerplays, singing games, folk songs, holiday songs, and rounds are included in this collection of 125 songs. Most are well known, traditional titles; others are modern songs. Useful features are the notes included for fingerplays and singing games and the song title and subject indexes. The lively color and black-and-white illustrations by Anita Lobel complement the songs and make this an exquisite and classic collection.

Hogstrom, Daphne. **My Big Book of Fingerplays: A Fun-to-Say, Fun-to-Play Collection**. il. by Sally Augustiny. Racine, Wis.: Western Publishing, 1974.

Hogstrom's book is an oversized collection of eighteen fingerplays and action rhymes. Sketches are used to indicate gestures, and the written directions are usually located near these sketches. Because the sketches and the written directions aren't right next to the rhymes, it takes a bit longer to understand how to do each activity. Don't let this or the uninspired illustrations put you off. These activities are original, clever, and fun for children to do. Action rhymes dominate the collection, and children particularly like them. These activities can be used in a wide range of programs, from "royalty" and "farms" to "circus" and "imagination."

Hunt, Mary Alice, ed. **A Multimedia Approach to Children's Literature: A Selective List of Films (and Videocassettes), Filmstrips and Recordings Based on Children's Books**, 3d ed. Chicago: American Library Association, 1983.

Use this book when you want to buy or borrow book-related nonprint material. This is a very selective collection arranged alphabetically by book title. Each book title is followed by film, filmstrip, and record versions of the book. You'll find helpful information, including brief annotations, age levels, playing times, and comments on music and narrator when they are particularly noteworthy. If you have a book that is too small to share with a group of children, check this source to see if a quality film or filmstrip version exists.

Lima, Carolyn W. **A to Zoo: Subject Access to Children's Picture Books**, 2d ed. New York: R. R. Bowker, 1986.

Lima's book is a comprehensive subject guide that lists book titles, arranged alphabetically by author, within subject headings. A separate index gives full bibliographic information for each book. Use this guide to lead you to titles on a specific subject. You can also quickly determine whether there are enough books to do a program on a subject you're considering. And you might see a book listed under a subject for which you never considered it. A word of caution: Use this book as a starting point because titles included span preschool through grade two. Without examining a specific title, you really can't tell if it will work in a story hour or not.

Mother Goose. **Tomie dePaola's Mother Goose**. il. by Tomie dePaola. New York: Putnam, 1985.

This is a beautifully illustrated collection of over two hundred Mother Goose rhymes. Many are well known; others are less familiar. You'll want to share the full-color paintings filled with humor and playfulness with your story hour group. Open your program with one of these poems; they fit into so many program subjects. Use your imagination, and turn some of these rhymes into fingerplays.

Olson, Margaret J. **Lots More Tell and Draw Stories**. Minneapolis, Minn.: Arts & Crafts Unlimited, 1973.

Olson, Margaret J. **More Tell and Draw Stories**. Minneapolis, Minn.: Arts & Crafts Unlimited, 1969.

Olson, Margaret J. **Tell and Draw Stories**. Minneapolis, Minn.: Creative Storytime press, 1963.

These books are clever collections of original short stories that you can tell and create on a chalkboard or a large piece of paper. The table of contents shows an illustration of what your finished creation will be next to the accompanying story title. This tells you at a glance in what program you can use an item. Each story has step-by-step drawings on the left side of the page keyed to the text. You'll find them easy to learn and execute.

Peterson, Carolyn Sue, and Brenny Hall. **Story Programs: A Source Book of Materials**. Metuchen, N.J.: Scarecrow, 1980.

You'll find ideas for programming with toddlers, preschoolers, and primary grade children in this book. The chapters on flannel board activities, creative dramatics, and puppetry are particularly useful. You'll find songs, poems, and stories with patterns for use as flannel board activities. In the puppetry chapter, you'll find verses, songs, stories, and plays to use with puppets. Patterns are included as well as direct instructions on how to make and work puppets.

In each chapter, check material for all age levels because some of the material in the sections devoted to toddlers and the primary level is appropriate to use with preschoolers.

Ring a Ring O' Roses: Stories, Games and Finger Plays for Pre-School Children, rev. ed. Flint, Mich.: Flint Public Library, 1981.

If you can only own one collection of fingerplays, purchase this small-format paperback. *Ring a Ring O' Roses* is probably the most comprehensive collection of its type. Over 450 fingerplays and action rhymes are divided by major headings and subheadings that are listed in the table of contents. Among the best sections are "Animal Kingdom," "Down on the Farm," "Holidays," "Child from Top to Toe," and "Things That Go." There are many counting rhymes that are quite successful with four and five year olds.

Scott, Louise Binder, and J. J. Thompson. **Rhymes for Fingers and Flannelboards**. il. by Jean Flowers. Minneapolis, Minn.: Webster Publishing/ T. S. Denison, 1960.

Some of the rhymes in this collection sound formal and outdated, but many are still entertaining to children. You'll find a number of useful fingerplays in the sections entitled "The Farm" and "The Seasons." "From Other Lands" is a unique collection of fingerplays in foreign languages, and the authors have included ideas for using many of the fingerplays in this collection on a flannelboard.

Sutherland, Zena. **Children and Books**, 7th ed. Glenview, Ill.: Scott, Foresman, 1986.

This is a comprehensive text about children's books. If you're new at evaluating and selecting children's books, then read the chapters entitled "Books for the Very Young," "Artists and Children's Books," and "Poetry." These discussions and the bibliographies that follow them give you a basic foundation from which you can build your knowledge of children's books. Consult the appendix entitled "Book Selection Aids" for other useful titles.